TEACH *from the* HEART

TEACH *from the* HEART

Pedagogy as Spiritual Practice

JENELL PARIS

CASCADE *Books* · Eugene, Oregon

TEACH FROM THE HEART
Pedagogy as Spiritual Practice

Cascade Books
An Imprint of Wipf and Stock Publishers
199 W. 8th Ave., Suite 3
Eugene, OR 97401

www.wipfandstock.com

PAPERBACK ISBN 13: 978-1-4982-3349-1
HARDCOVER ISBN 13: 978-1-4982-3351-4
EBOOK ISBN: 978-1-4982-3350-7

Cataloguing-in-Publication data:

Name: Paris, Jenell.

Title: Teach from the heart: Pedagogy as spiritual practice/ Jenell Paris.

Description: Eugene, OR: Cascade Books, 2016 | Includes bibliographical references.

Identifiers: ISBN 978-1-4982-3349-1 (paperback) | ISBN 978-1-4982-3351-4 (hardcover) | ISBN 978-1-4982-3350-7 (ebook)

Subjects: LCSH: Teaching. | Learning. | Teachers. | Title.

Classification: LB1025 .P225 2016 (print) | LB1025 (ebook)

Manufactured in the USA.   06/23/16 for Janel and Alison

I sing the praise of the unknown teacher.

Great generals win campaigns, but it is the unknown soldier who wins the war.

Famous educators plan new systems of pedagogy, but it is the unknown teacher who delivers and guides the young. He lives in obscurity and contends with hardship. For him no trumpets blare, no chariots wait, no golden decorations are decreed. He keeps watch along the borders of darkness and makes the attack on the trenches of ignorance and folly. Patient in his daily duty, he strives to conquer the evil powers which are the enemies of youth. He awakens sleeping spirits. He quickens the indolent, encourages the eager, and steadies the unstable. He communicates his own joy in learning and shares with boys and girls the best treasure of his mind. He lights many candles which, in later years, will shine back to cheer him. This is his reward.

Knowledge may be gained from books; but the love of knowledge is transmitted only by personal contact. No one has deserved better of the republic than the unknown teacher. No one is more worthy to be enrolled in a democratic aristocracy, "king of himself and servant of mankind."

—Henry Van Dyke (1852–1933)[1]

---

1. Van Dyke, "The Unknown Teacher," iv.

Contents

Acknowledgments

This book began as a sabbatical project, and I am grateful to Messiah College for granting the sabbatical. I wrote at the Collegeville Institute of St. John's University in Collegeville, Minnesota. The birds, dragonflies, grasshoppers, and bees mentioned in this book are those of Stumpf Lake, along the walking trail that provided me an inspirational commute. My family enjoyed the Benedictine hospitality of the monks and staff of the Institute, especially Don Ottenhoff, Carla Durand, and Janel Kragt Bakker. Janel companioned me through writing this book, and we discovered mutual interests for other projects. I see the benefits of her editorial eye and spiritual mind throughout the book.

My sister-in-law, Jessica Paris Wheeler, helps me expand what seems possible in my voice, audience, and purpose.

My spiritual director, Nancy Linton, blesses me in every way, including encouragement in writing.

My writer's group, Pinklings, contributed to every stage of the process, from brainstorming to careful reviewing to advice on titles. Thank you to Leah Clarke, Crystal Downing, Meg Ramey, Kate Simcox, Val Weaver-Zercher, and Cynthia Wells.

Many teachers appear in these pages, some former teachers of mine and some current colleagues, many in composite or pseudonymous form. I found an eighth grade paper on which Ms. Sasse had written, "You could be a writer!" Nearly three decades later, I dug out that paper and received her words again as I wrote this book. Thanks also to Mary Ellen Ashcroft, Ray Barfield, Jimmy Barnhill, Dave Bartelmas, Heather Barto, Greg Boyd, Kevin Cragg, Timothy Essenberg, Margot Eyring, Steve Garber, Ken Gowdy, Jerry Herbert, Michael Holmes, James Hurd, Margie Koch, William Leap, Neil and Virginia Lettinga, Alison Noble, Meg Ramey, Harley Schreck, Hannah Tims, Brett Williams, and Samuel Zalanga.

Students provided vital feedback, review, editorial support, and no end of stories. Thanks to Elizabeth Erasquin-Nethery, Drew Gehman, Elisabeth Ivey, Lynette Mhangami, Kate Miller, Ben Olson, and Hannah Ruth.

Above the shelf in my office where I store my own journals, drafts, and publications, I keep a shelf of authors who "oversee" my work. Thanks to Elizabeth Andrew, Annie Dillard, Thich Nhat Hanh, David M. Levy, Margaret Mead, Karen Maezen Miller, Kathleen Norris, Mary Oliver, Mary Rose O'Reilley, Neil Postman, Rumi, Howard Thurman, and Simone Weil.

My children provided me with every possible distraction from writing, and I'm grateful that they didn't let me miss their lives unfolding. Thank you for that, Wesley, Oliver, and Maxwell. Thank you, James, for encouraging me to reclaim my teacherly ideals, refashion them for these middle years of my career, and believe it possible to live into them. And for making breakfast.

Introduction

This book is for teachers. It offers encouragement for sustaining a rich inner life so that the passion that drew you into teaching can carry you all the way through, even as you accumulate the dents, scars, and wrinkles that come with strenuous and sustained work. It is about finding, rediscovering, and holding on to the heart of the teaching life, which is the seat of passion, or the sacred center; in short, the teacher's heart. It is an encouragement to take up teaching as more than a service to provide, a profession to master, or a job to perform. It is an invitation to artisanry, to honor teaching as a craft that we master by working with our hands over long periods of time, producing results that bear the mark of their maker.

I write to inspire us teachers to hold on to our highest hopes that our work matters, a monumental challenge in a time when economic and political changes are diminishing teachers' freedom to explore, create, and wonder with our students. This is a pedagogy of love for fearful times, a way of teaching and learning that both tells the truth about our fears, and shapes us to respond in wise and helpful ways. It's not a technique or a set of best practices that can be downloaded and implemented: problem solved. It isn't about becoming a better teacher, or even a better person. It is a way—a path, an invitation—to become more fully who you already are, to trust that you are good enough, and to share your real and true self with your students.

> In a teacher's coming to understand himself, in his becoming a person,
> he comes to be a more effective teacher.
>
> —LUIZ NATALICIO[2]

    I write to remind teachers, including myself, that who we are is good enough. This doesn't mean we have achieved greatness or perfection; rather, it means that our humanity, as it is, is sufficient for the task. Our shortcomings, and the ways we integrate our flaws and limits into our professional practice, shows students how to be tenacious learners and whole human beings. Being a good student isn't about earning all As, or mastering material easily and quickly, showcasing your strengths and tucking away the mistakes. In fact, I worry about my students with 4.0 GPAs—that they can perform better than they can learn. More often, it's the student with the 3.0, the 2.5, even the 1.7 GPA, who has tried and failed, or tried not trying at all, who is learning a lot: learning her limits, learning what matters and what doesn't, and learning how to come back after failure. It is not perfection, but risk-taking and resilience that makes a strong learner, be that learner a student or a teacher.

Chapters arc from fear to love, roaming across the terrain of the teaching life to reflect on topics including mindfulness, academic integrity, boundaries with students, and teaching with joy and love. Each chapter offers a practice, one that can be drawn down into any teaching context: stories are drawn from preschool, K–12, and community education, and from my primary context of college teaching. The practices are not religious ones accessible only to adherents: they are ordinary, everyday acts of teaching, the things we have to do anyway, but that we can choose to do mindfully, with loving attention and devotion.

    Stories come from colleagues, friends, teachers at seminars I've taught or attended, and students of all ages. Many are from my experience, spanning the schools I've been part of either as student or as teacher, in California, Minnesota, Pennsylvania, and Washington, DC. Most names and details are altered to preserve anonymity, with the exception of a few individuals who granted permission for their names and stories to appear here.

---

2. Natalicio and Hereford, *The Teacher as a Person*, ix.

My student self always comes with me to class: the kindergartener who cried, the seventh grader who wanted to become a writer, the senior who skipped class because she just wanted to be done with high school already, and the graduate student who wanted to get everything perfect. These past selves remind me of how a teacher's comment, glance, or note on an assignment may have long-lasting influence. Some stories are from my K–12 education at public schools in Minneapolis suburbs, with the exception of K–1 in Fresno, CA. I went to college at Bethel University in St. Paul, Minnesota, a liberal arts college rooted in the Baptist tradition, where I majored in Sociology and Anthropology, and minored in Economics. In graduate school at American University in Washington, DC, I was both student and teacher, sometimes serving as graduate assistant or instructor for undergraduate classes as I worked toward my PhD in Anthropology.

Teaching is at the heart of my professional passion and purpose, yet I've never taken an education class. Like most college professors, I studied deeply in my discipline and learned the skills of a scholar—to research, write, and publish—through explicit instruction. I learned to become a teacher through more implicit means: by observation, trial and error, and reflection on my own experiences as a student. I served as teaching assistant to various professors, and shaped my teaching practice in response to what I observed in them, a modern form of apprenticeship. My first teaching position was at the American Studies Program in Washington, DC, a semester program for Christian college students. Next, I taught at Bethel University, my alma mater, for eight years, and now I teach at Messiah College in Grantham, Pennsylvania, a liberal arts college that is actively religious in the Wesleyan, Anabaptist, and Pietist traditions. Away from my paid employment, I also teach a card-making class in a community education program, volunteer in my children's public school classrooms, and tutor an individual child.

Ms. Thomas, my twins' first grade teacher, quieted her class with clapping. She'd clap a rhythm, SLOW-SLOW-QUICK-QUICK-QUICK, and the kids knew to respond with the same, SLOW-SLOW-QUICK-QUICK-QUICK. I tried it at home and my boys rolled their eyes. "That only works at school, Mom." Teachers clap, ring chimes, shake maracas, flicker light switches, and raise our voices; whatever it takes to get our students to quiet down and pay attention. It's good advice for us teachers, too.

Teachers, too, should pay attention in class, not only to students and their learning, but to ourselves and how the work of teaching shapes us as human beings. Approaching the classroom as a sacred space for our formation as teachers and as persons enables us to bring more peace, gentleness, kindness, and love into the world by growing these fruits in ourselves, sharing them with our students, and sending our students out into the world.

1

The Change You Wish to See

Be the change you wish to see in the world.

—GANDHI

At a recent college commencement I sat with the faculty, each of us decked out in heavy regalia and sweating under a bright Pennsylvania sun, wondering whether the commencement speaker would keep his promise of speaking for less than twelve minutes.

"Students," he said, "you're beginning your adult lives in a world worthy of your fear. You're facing economic decline, the worst job market in decades, years of ongoing wars, vitriolic political and public speech, mass shootings, and violence."

Shouldn't a commencement speech inspire? I wondered. *Seems like a downer.*

His message rang true, though, in both content and length (eleven minutes). Students are learning, and we are teaching, in a time worthy of our fear.

College students fear, and rightfully so, that:

- in the short run, there won't be enough jobs, or enough good jobs. The financial discrepancy between college investment and earning potential in the near future may prove severe.

- in the long run, they won't achieve a standard of living even equal to that of their parents.

- the music, sports, extra curriculars, and part-time jobs that populate their resumes won't be enough.

- their webs of relationships will be thick and omnipresent online, but lonely and thin in everyday life.

- the political, economic, and environmental webs in which their lives are suspended are tenuous, unstable, and too often corrupt.

These aren't only the fears of young adulthood, just dawning on new college graduates. They came up through K–12 with all this plus test anxiety, pressure to succeed, fear of violence and bullying, and exquisite awareness of natural disaster, war, and environmental threats on a global level.[1]

Even preschoolers show signs of stress and fear due to rapid and unexpected change in their environments, frequent changes in caregivers, and family economic conditions.[2] Poverty is stressful in many ways, but wealth can also be fear inducing, when preschool admission becomes a high-stakes endeavor that threatens to derail a toddler's life trajectory.

Teachers and institutional leaders fear, and rightfully so, that:

- the political, economic, and regulatory systems that support education are too broken, and on all levels: national, state, local, and interpersonal.

- they can only do so much work, yet the load is ever-increasing, for those who still have, or manage to get, full-time teaching jobs.

- there won't be—*there already are not*—enough financial and human resources to run our schools with excellence, or even just to keep the doors open.

- there could be—*there already is*—violence on campus at any moment and without warning.

- the systems we use to evaluate and promote students, schools, and teachers aren't just; in fact, they are sometimes dysfunctional to the

---

1. "National Poll on Children's Health."
2. "Booklet for Parents."

point of counterproductivity, miseducating students and turning teachers cynical.

- we have little time to think, read, or write. We work on electronic communication constantly, with expectations for extremely rapid reply. One of my students recently complained, "It's impossible to track you down," after his email went unanswered for twenty minutes! We invest more time and energy learning new technology modalities and software than we spend keeping up with our disciplines.

- education is facing a crisis of unprecedented proportion, unless it isn't, and the language of crisis is being used to sell books, redistribute resources at schools, and cow us into submission.

Personally, as a professor with nearly twenty years of teaching under my belt and at least that many more ahead of me, and as a parent with three children in public schools, I worry:

- are teachers becoming little more than educational service providers? Are we not artisans, artists, and journeymen; masters of a trade that we practice with nuance, intuition, and idiosyncrasy? Will the assessors, the regulators, and the bean counters make service workers of us all?

- can we teachers work in happiness and well-being? Can we be whole, healthy, happy, and kind, even as we, our children, and our neighbors' children are immersed in and sustained by educational systems that are broken, sometimes to sadistic proportions?

- can the idealism that got us into teaching last an entire career? I started teaching with high hopes, bright balloons on strings I held in my hand. It seemed possible to delight in my students and they in me, to be an active and progressive participant in my college, to be one among millions of educators that are valued and respected by society. Each of those ideals has been challenged by reality, often painfully. Is it inevitable that those strings will slip from my grip, balloons floating away out of sight?

And what would become of me then, teaching anthropology—the study of the human experience—when my own humanity has been burned out or shriveled up? Parker Palmer warns, "When our fears as teachers mingle and multiply with the fears of our students, teaching and learning become mechanical, manipulative, lifeless."[3]

If the titles of recent books about American education are any indication, doom is the only possible future. Teachers and students are *adrift, failing, wasting,* and *underachieving.* We are *losing our minds* (our *closed minds*). We have already *lost our soul.* American education is *imploding, exploding, on the brink, at the end.* It is a time of *crisis, death.* These themes spin out in various directions, depending on vantage point and ideological persuasion, arrows of blame slung at teachers, parents, administrators, politicians, unions, or larger forces such as neoliberalism.

The commencement speaker took a different turn. He turned to a phrase from the Bible, "There is no fear in love, but perfect love casts out fear" (I John 4:18, ESV). Fear goads us to be defensive, reactive, and on edge, but after we do defensive and reactive things, we still feel afraid, and we've likely created more reasons for others to fear. Love is gentle, generous, and kind, and it diminishes fear in very practical ways. It empowers us to act with courage at center stage, fear present but in the wings; to take on the tangled messes that diminish student learning, even to take on the difficult people in our everyday lives, from a place other than the alarm and unease that such problems tell us is inescapable.

"Go out into the world," the speaker said, "go out into the rest of your lives, and love. Love a lot, love freely, love everybody. Try it and see if it's true, that perfect love casts out fear."

The social conditions that precipitate our fears need description and analysis, but naming them isn't sufficient. Describing them in great detail and assigning blame for their origin and persistence, isn't sufficient. Fear carries strong energy that needs direction. Directing it toward vitriolic speech, xenophobia, war, hateful political engagement, or survivalist withdrawal is short-sighted at best; at worst, it is destructive of the social contract.

Cultivating more love, within ourselves and in our classrooms and our schools, strengthens a wind pattern, a channel for fear to flow through our lives and through the world without consuming everything in sight. It enables us to discuss our fears and construct considered and efficacious responses and strategies for change. My hope is that it can even cast out fear, or at least diminish it enough so that we can teach for years and years with sustainable enthusiasm, happiness, and hope, balloon strings firm in hand.

3. Palmer, "Good Teaching," 16.

Many (most, dare I say) teachers have spiritual sensitivity; after all, like social work or nursing, one doesn't go into teaching to get rich, to be famous, or to hurt people. Though they can become distorted, deflated, or forgotten over time, most of us start out with noble purposes and high ideals; at the very least, that there is something more to life than making money and spending it, and that investing in students matters.

Spirituality in the teaching life is the unmistakable spark that makes a teacher wise, joyous, and fully alive. It isn't about being, or becoming, religious; rather, it's an invitation to a journey of the heart, many dimensions of which may be appropriately shared or integrated into classrooms in a pluralist society, a journey stemming from and contributing to the liberal arts tradition. While he honors the separation of public education from religion, educator Parker Palmer also encourages soul education, which begins with nurture of teachers' inner lives. "A teacher has the power to compel students to spend many hours living in the light, or the shadow, of the teacher's inner life."[4] As English professor Barbara Newman writes,

> I'm paid to teach English in a secular university. But I believe the formation of contemplative habits and the reduction of mental clutter are goods in themselves, so nothing keeps me from promoting such goods, as long as they remain ancillary to the study of literature. This privilege comes with getting too old to be cool and *way* too old to be "hot," as Rate My Professors has it. If teachers of a certain age don't try to teach wisdom, with heart and mind and soul and strength—then who will?[5]

Writing in English, and in a western frame of mind, limits my ability to speak of spirituality. It can connote religion, which makes it unsuitable for many classrooms and many teachers. It can connote a woo-woo, kumbaya vibe that is also unhelpful for many subjects, schools, and teachers. What I'm getting at is something like the *a!ia* of the Ju/'hoansi, an indigenous group in southern Africa. Traditionally, *a!ia* referred to a hot energy that boils up from the stomach and comes out the hands of a healer, drawing sickness and malevolence out of people. Before they became more familiar with the broader world, they also used the word to refer to aircraft contrails or radios. *A!ia* is a fantastic presence that surprises even while it is not

4. Palmer, "Teaching with Heart and Soul," 378.
5. Newman, "Contemplative Classroom," 4.

unexpected.[6] It is something like the realm accessed by Yanamamo men when they forcibly blow *ebene*, a hallucinogenic powder, into each others' sinus cavities, producing an altered state that allows them to draw *hekura* into their own bodies, the spirits that reside in every single vine, tree, animal, and living thing.[7]

The Ju/'hoansi *a!ia* is hardly the same thing as the Yąnamamo hallucinogenic state, which is different than the Christian's Holy Spirit, prayer, or contemplation, the Buddhist's Buddhahood, or the Sufi's *ihsan*, perfection of worship. What I have in mind—surely not precisely the same as, but in the vicinity of what these examples bear witness to—is not principally special, not beyond, other than, or more than. It's mere immanence, which is sheer immanence. It is already there, already within, but still, a gift when we see it. It is the iridescence of everyday life.

I've said too much, like my son who ran into the woods recently shouting, "I'll play my recorder for the birds, and they will come to me!" There was stomping and more shouting, followed by piercing squeaks of various tones. This was followed by no bird sightings whatsoever. Much later, when we weren't looking but were ready to see, they came: birds, lots of them, along with dragonflies, grasshoppers, bees, and even a snake.

I'm a glutton for spirituality: as an anthropologist, I'm fascinated by the ways people explore the whole universe, parts visible and invisible. Personally, I've been deeply involved in Protestant Christianity since birth, in fundamentalist, evangelical, Holiness, and Anabaptist communities, and am currently part of a United Methodist congregation. I read Zen Buddhism and practice mindfulness meditation, but I wouldn't call myself Buddhist; I don't have a teacher or a *sangha* (community), and I only read Buddhism made palatable for Western readers. Inspired by animist cultures I've studied, I expect to encounter the sacred everywhere, in any living or natural thing. I follow the way of Jesus, who said, "Look at the birds of the air," and "See how the flowers of the field grow" (Matt 6:25–34). I look and see the sacred, *a!ia*, everywhere.

We can recognize this sacred dimension of life in the classroom, too. English professor Mary Rose O'Reilley observes, "Some pedagogical practices crush the soul; most of us have suffered their bruising force. Others allow the spirit to come home: to self, to community, and to the revelations of

6. Lee, *Dobe Ju/'hoansi*.

7. Chagnon, *Yąnamamö*.

reality."[8] Such practices constitute what she calls "radical presence," a contemplative, focused, sensory approach to learning that involves attunement to self and other, listening and watching closely. Her techniques are suited to her personality and to her subject. She sends students out into nature to sit still and observe, and write about something they observed. She reads a poem in class, then allows ninety seconds of silence before speaking. The techniques don't necessarily translate into my anthropology classroom, with its more empirical and social scientific approach to investigating the human experience, nor to my teaching temperament. But the way—shaping an educational space for students that encourages presence, attention, and deep learning—is one I want to follow.

Whether conceptualized as contemplative pedagogy, mindfulness, or an application of a specific religious tradition, interest in this way is growing. From preschools to colleges to graduate schools, teachers are increasingly interested in how to strengthen, deepen, broaden, and enliven their students' education by teaching to, and from, the heart.[9]

I enjoyed such a discussion recently when I taught a faculty development seminar. This was a religious college, so the notion of integrating faith and learning is easily valued by teachers because it is a central part of the college's mission. In this exercise, however, we intentionally separated "religious" from "ordinary" so spirituality could remain full and free, related to but not subordinated to religion. The question at hand was, what practices do, or could, keep you whole and happy, able to teach well for an entire semester, an entire year, an entire career?

I've filled in the chart with some of their responses. I noticed teachers easily identifying religious practices as spiritually meaningful, but it was more difficult to value "ordinary" practices in such a lofty way. When someone mentioned sleep, however, the room filled with laughter. Though it is invisible to students, and it may not seem very spiritual or religious, getting enough rest during the semester is absolutely vital for teaching well. Many practices benefit both student and teacher, though in different ways.

Practices are concrete actions we do as part of some community, be it a sports team, a neighborhood, a religion, or a profession. Craig Dykstra

---

8. O'Reilley, *Radical Presence*, 3.

9. See organizations such as the Center for Action and Contemplation, the Center for Courage and Renewal, the Association for Contemplation in Higher Education, and the Center for Contemplative Mind in Society.

and Dorothy Bass explain, "One thing about practices is that they are very down-to-earth. When people engage in a practice, they don't just talk about it, though words often play an important part. People at practice do things."[10] Our habits, talents, and values are shaped by how we practice.

We become more deeply connected to our community through shared practices. In teaching, this is a challenge because we are often alone in the classroom with our students. Despite the presence of students, and the existence of millions of other teachers in society, classroom teaching is often a solo performance. Teachers can be very guarded in talking with other teachers about teaching, both for reasons of personal pride or embarrassment, or because of assessment and promotion processes. When schools provide safe spaces for deep conversation about teaching, or when teachers seek out such spaces through friendship, professional conferences, or other venues, teachers may find relief, connection with others, and both professional and personal rejuvenation through vulnerable and purposeful self-reflection on their teaching practice.

10. Dykstra and Bass, *Practicing our Faith*, 9.

	Spiritual practices that are also religious	Everyday spiritual practices
Visible to students	Praying in class Using religious examples in lectures Offering stories from the teacher's faith journey Using stories from sacred texts to illustrate class concepts	Eye contact Learning students' names Sending progress reports even when not required Smiling Giving gifts to students: stickers, treats, erasers Integrating personal anecdotes that help students feel connected to me Restraining myself from using Facebook or email during class Doing my class prep or scholarship in the school library, in view of students
Invisible to students	Community service done with church Personal prayer, study of sacred texts Church attendance Worship	Family time Sleep Nutrition Recreation and leisure Studying student names and photos outside of class Pausing, or meditating, for a few minutes before class starts to gain focus Setting aside enough time to grade well, and doing it in a well-chosen spot

I had set up the seminar for the teachers, of course, but also for self-interested reasons. I wanted to hear their answers so I could strengthen the sustainability of my own teaching life. Nearly all these ideas inspired me, but how would I add anything more to my teaching practice? I have classes to teach, papers to grade, committee work to do, and so on. And I have a family: mouths to feed, laundry to fold, and a cat box to clean. Like millions of other teachers who are also parents (my three boys are in early elementary grades), there is no margin in my life to add something more, or to overhaul my approach to teaching, or to rewrite my curriculum or class plans. I have to practice right where I am, where I have to be anyway, which is in my usual classroom, teaching the usual subjects, with my usual students.

One evening as I encouraged my three sons to pay attention to their schoolwork, I realized I could do the same with my own. I folded a few pieces of paper, stapled the crease, and asked Oliver to decorate the cover, a red piece of paper with a label that reads, in his second-grade block letters, "HIGH LOW." The left side of each paper is for "highs" and the right side is for "lows." High-low is a family practice; we do it each night before bed, each boy and parent reflecting on their day. Personal highs often involve a victory at recess or a good dessert, and lows are often kicks, scrapes, and wounds inflicted by a brother or by asphalt.

This practice is inspired by St. Ignatius of Loyola, a sixteenth-century Spanish knight who, during a period of convalescence following severe battle wounds, turned to God. He wrote the *Spiritual Exercises*, practices followed by the order he founded, the Jesuits. One of these exercises calls for daily reflection on consolations and desolations—it's less daunting to call them "highs and lows." It isn't mere pleasure and pain. Lows drain us of energy, take us inward and down, and cut us off from friendship, service, and community. Highs strengthen our energy, tie us to others in generative community, and broaden and lift our view.

For two years, at the end of each work day, I spent about one minute reflecting on the high and low of my work day and I wrote a phrase—never as much as a sentence—in my journal. Highs might be "talking with a student about her life" or "reading a book." Lows included "too many emails," and "ran out of steam in class, and the book I assigned is awful." Over time I began to see patterns in what enlivens my spirit and what depresses it. These patterns were sometimes unexpected: for example, confronting an unrepentant student about plagiarism was one high. She was belligerent and deflected responsibility—*If you had taught me how to write better, I wouldn't have had to copy from that book.* Nonetheless, I felt alive in the clarity of the moment and in my capacity to take responsibility, and I was proud to be able to offer her a meaningful opportunity to get back on course. One of my persistent lows was being tired. I almost always get tired in the early afternoon, but I hadn't realized it was a pattern; instead, I'd downplay it and push myself through with candy and caffeine. Recognizing it helped me find other ways to cope, the best being a ten-minute nap under my desk or outside under a tree.

High-low helps me notice, without judgment or attempting to change it, my anger, impatience, disregard, stress, and jealousy, the many ways in which I carry and perpetuate the worst of my guild, profession, and society. I also notice joy, peace, kindness, self-control, delight, fun, laughter, and longing, and appreciate how they often seem to just appear, unbidden. The goal is not to get more highs and fewer lows, but to notice them all, let them be, and hold them with compassion. Ignatius taught that our spirits can grow and be strengthened in both consolation and desolation, but they must be recognized and treated according to their nature. This is similar to the principle of mindfulness currently popular in self-help literature: "to be aware of what is happening in our present experiences, observing with compassion, insight, and an intention to create joy."[11]

It also helped me realize that my daily life that grounds me in a full-time job and a family is not an anchor holding me back from exploring and deepening my inner life; rather, it is my ticket for doing so. I don't need to add pilgrimage, retreats, a labyrinth, or other spiritual undertakings, because I already have a host of spiritual practices that are distinctive, rigorous, and life-shaping, such as course preparation, grading, student discipline, collegiality with other teachers, and navigating the school bureaucracy. At home, there are abundant opportunities in parenting, cooking, cleaning, doing laundry, and being a partner to my husband. I don't always see them as such, but when I pay attention, the spirits come into view. Sometimes *alia* appears in fantastic and extraordinary ways. More often, the days and moments are ordinary ones in which the animating spirits of the curriculum, the classroom, the students, or the teacher come into view.

Whether or not we intend to teach from the heart, we all do. Whether or not we mean for students to notice, they do. For better and for worse, the inner lives of teachers affect students. As Ralph Waldo Emerson wrote, "If a teacher have any opinion which he wishes to conceal, his pupils will

---

11. Rotne and Rotne, *Everybody Present*, 21.

become as fully indoctrinated into that as into any which he publishes . . . . Show us an arc of the curve, and a good mathematician will find out the whole figure."[12] My friend Angie echoed this sentiment when she reflected on her forty years teaching middle school. She said, "Teaching isn't just a skill. It's a way of being. Who I am, how I am, as a person . . . that's who I am with my students." This comment came in the middle of a story about a kid who pushed her buttons. She remembered him with regret, "He sure got to me, but I never reached him." She remembers the ones who got away, and hopes they connected with other teachers.

We don't just teach what we know. We teach who we are. Sixty years ago, education reformer Frances F. Fuller wrote, "Teachers teach far more than just intellectual content in their total interactions with students. Students learn from teachers' attitudes and ways of responding which comprise part of their ability to cope, but which teachers may not be conscious of teaching . . . . To adapt an adage, ofttimes what teachers *are* speaks so loudly that students cannot hear what they say."[13]

Thus, education should include and exceed technical mastery and job attainment, such that the well-educated person enjoys a more rich and liberated life, one that, by necessity, spills over in blessing to other people and to the whole world. In various ways and with distinctives drawn from their individual traditions, students and teachers alike become the change they have read about, and have come to long for, in the world.

Consider just a few of the dozens of course objectives I've written in syllabi for anthropology, gender studies, and urban studies classes:

- to understand and appreciate the influence of culture in the human experience.

- to explore how culture impacts our consciousness, experience, and display of gender and sexual identity.

- to gain confidence and skills in speaking and listening to public discourse about race and ethnicity.

- to pursue career and vocational exploration and choices.

Years ago I learned this material sufficient to earn a doctorate, but I haven't come close to mastering my own course objectives, to say nothing

12. Emerson, "Spiritual Laws."
13. Fuller, "Intensive Individualization," 3.

of the vastness of my discipline. An Introduction to Cultural Anthropology student asked, "How many times have you taught this class?"

"I think this is my twenty-first or twenty-second time," I answered.

"Don't you get bored?"

"No," I replied, "because this is my first time teaching *this* class. You were never there before—that's a first. And the field of anthropology is always changing, and this class reminds me to try to keep up."

I enroll in my own classes over and over, hoping to make a little more progress toward understanding the world and my place in it, the diverse ways of humankind, and the ways of my society. At our best, teachers are more than brains in search of data. We are human beings on a quest for wisdom, and have attained enough to share with others. World religions pass on stories of teachers of the law, or judges, who lack wisdom. They interpret law too literally, or with favor and bias. They may know the letter of the law, but fail to embody and transmit its spirit. Whether religious law, anthropology, or math, teaching is not just about knowing *that*, but knowing *why, when,* and *for whom.*

The stakes are high. Our students go out into the world, influenced by us for better and for worse. My former students are resettling refugees, managing nonprofits, teaching English, and raising families, among many other pursuits. It would be nice if, years after they graduate, they could remember my lectures about Ulrich Zwingli's reforms in Switzerland, or Waorani sorcery, but most of them won't. It's essential, however, that they are more loving, kind, and generous, more focused and purposeful, and more skilled and capable, for having spent hundreds of hours in class with teachers.

2

Your Attention Please

To pay attention, this is our endless and proper work.

—MARY OLIVER, *WHITE PINE*

I wasn't paying attention. Jet lag, long days, and the stress of being responsible for twenty-five American undergraduates in Amsterdam got the better of me. At any given moment in the first days of this international urban studies course, I might forget what time zone we were in, or lead the group down the wrong street. At the end of a long day I was relieved to be alone in my room, ready for bed. I unlaced my hiking boots and kicked them under the bed. Took off my corduroys and left them where they fell. Pulled my sweater over my head.

Suddenly I heard shouts and banging on my door. I couldn't distinguish one voice from another, but I got the point. "Stop, Dr. Paris! We can see you!"

I leaped back into my clothes, cracked the door, and saw five of my female students. I was mortified, too embarrassed to even open my door all the way. "Omigosh, thanks," I mumbled, closing the door to hide out for the night. My room was in the curve of a U-shaped dormitory, and I had failed to notice that my room could be seen from any other along both legs of the U, and my curtains were open.

We teachers often encourage students to pay attention in class, and when encouragement doesn't do it, we lure, cajole, insist, and command. In one of my childhood classrooms, the clock was just above and behind Mr. Stevens, who didn't allow us to look at it. Each time he saw a student's eyes wander upward from his face, he'd call the student out by name and threaten to call his or her parents. In college, Professor Otto littered his lectures with jokes just to keep us listening. He'd open a semester by standing in front of the class looking confused, and then quip, "I feel like a mosquito in a nudist colony: I don't know where to start."

Attention derives from the French *attendre*, to expect or to wait for. Literally, it means to stretch toward.[1] Class attendance is about more than rear ends in chairs, whether in a physical classroom or in front of a computer for an online class. It's about attending to the class, stretching one's mind toward the material, waiting in expectation for something valuable.

Teachers can't come in late, slump back in a back row seat with baseball cap over eyes, or shop for Spring Break plane tickets while pretending to take notes (or not even bothering to pretend). But we can, and do, teach with attention that is less than rapt. When I looked over my high-low journal, some of my "lows" are along the lines of, "Why am I teaching such unimportant stuff?" and "I want to go home and take a nap." We may cover the material without uncovering the wonder of the subject. We may evaluate student performance without valuing or understanding student lives. We may display what we know, but not allow students to watch us explore what we don't know. We may answer questions important to us, but forget to entertain, or even to call forth, the questions students are asking.

Students see us standing in front of the class, but do they see us stretching? They see what we've mastered and learned, but do they see what we're waiting for, what we're expecting? When we're paying attention in class, we're *tending*, like gardeners or shepherds; caring for, working on, waiting for, stretching toward.

The classroom need not be merely a destination where we display for students what we've learned elsewhere. It can be a sacred space, a spiritual landscape for students and teachers to actively tend our lives and the life of the world. We could even take students as our spiritual guides, not by virtue of their greater wisdom or even their intention, but simply because they are present (or absent, as the case may be). By their presence, students

1. Online Etymology Dictioanry, "Attend."

offer daily opportunities for us to practice patience, gentleness, generosity, self-control, and all other virtues. The invitation is for us to be present, too, not only to the material but to our own experience of teaching.

In fact, perhaps attention itself is even more important than the academic subject at hand. French mystic Simone Weil explains that whether or not it results in mastery or even accurate understanding, attention itself orients the student toward the sacred.

> Attention consists of suspending our thought, leaving it detached, empty, and ready to be penetrated by the object; it means holding in our minds, within reach of this thought, but on a lower level and not in contact with it, the diverse knowledge we have acquired which we are forced to make use of . . . . Above all our thought should be empty, waiting, not seeking anything, but ready to receive in its naked truth the object that is to penetrate it.[2]

For teachers, such rigorous attention means making use of technique, technology, and disciplinary expertise, but not as mere technique, rather, with an open and expectant eye for what is really happening in our classroom, including what is happening to us. We need to fill up our schedules, our classrooms, and our curricula with purposeful activity, but also protect the emptiness that deep receptivity and learning requires. The outcome may not be as decisive as a mathematical proof or a grade on a quiz, but reward is certain.

> If there is a real desire, if the thing desired is really light, the desire for light produces it. There is a real desire when there is an effort of attention . . . . Even if our efforts of attention seem for years to be producing no result, one day a light that is in exact proportion to them will flood the soul. Every effort adds a little gold to a treasure no power on earth can take away.[3]

2. Weil, *Waiting for God*, 111–12.
3. Ibid., 107–8.

> I suggest that certain "spiritual disciplines" are available to us among the accepted practices of academic life—if only we would see them and use them as such. The core academic activities of teaching and research offer us many opportunities to open the inward space in which we can practice obedience to truth . . . .
>
> —PARKER PALMER[4]

For some, this spiritual journey is also religious: when the structures and traditions of religion facilitate wholeness of the human spirit, the harmony between religion and spirituality is fantastic. That is often not the case, and religion provides distraction, false rewards, or even destructive abuses of power. For most teachers, their curriculum and/or their lives are not set in the context of a religious tradition. Regardless, there's always a fuller meaning to the curriculum, whether the content is math, preliteracy, neurosurgery, or crafting. The fuller expression is the *why* of an educated life, the *why* that directs and gives meaning to the *how* of content and skill mastery. It's about focus and purpose, a more liberated and reflective human existence, devoted to increasing happiness and well-being in the world for all people and for the planet.

At a seminar I presented the notion of classroom as sacred space. An audience member, a loved and lovely faculty member who has been teaching (seemingly) over a hundred years raised his hand.

"This sounds like you're going backwards in time. We used to be focused on teaching, but now it's all about student learning. Shouldn't you put students at the center, instead of yourself?"

Is the center so small that only students or teacher can occupy that space? Of course we need to focus on students and their learning styles and challenges, and on pedagogies of learning and assessment. Caring also for the teacher's own self is not self-centered: when we don't, we damage ourselves and damage our students. We hide, withdrawing from struggles toward institutional change or even self-improvement in favor of mere survival. We waste energy complaining instead of mobilizing, gossiping instead of planning, and small-ball politicking instead of working effectively up to, and often against, the limits of the systems we're engaging. We

---

4. Palmer, *To Know as We Are Known*, 116.

17

use arrogance and jargon-filled monologue as a shield against our personal or intellectual limits being seen by students. We turn cynical, disgusted, and paranoid toward administrators, colleagues, and sometimes toward students. I remember one colleague saying, "I made a vow fifteen years ago never to talk to any administrator for any reason, and I've kept it." Another, explaining how he publishes so many books, says, "I don't give out my phone number, and I tell the students on the first day of class, you can email me only if you're on fire, and you've already tried someone else."

Instead of choosing student or teacher, teaching or learning, we can just expand the center (it's just a metaphorical center, after all), or take a fresh look and see how spacious it is and always was. When we do, we find that class can be as good for us as we hope it is for students, a place for all of us to learn and develop in preparation for the rest of our lives.

When a teacher insists on continuing to learn, and opens her heart to being changed and shaped each year with students, she is being the change she wishes to see in the world. This commitment, in however small a way, holds open the possibility for something better than the business model of education. The business model, dominant since the 1990s, says education is a purchasable service, students and their tax- or tuition-paying parents are consumers, and teachers are service providers. Chronicle Research Services issued a report on *The College of 2020*, predicting that, "Good teaching will always be at the core of a good university, but for most colleges, higher education will become a more retail-based industry than it ever has been. The students of the future will demand it."[5] Veteran urban educator Jeanine Molloff rails against the corporatization of K–12 education via standardized testing, endless documentation, and corporate partnerships with charter schools, food services, fund raisers, school photos, and media. "The agenda looks like reform, but its true direction is total corporate control."[6] Historian Jackson Lears warns, "The conquest of educational discourse by market models is nearly complete."[7]

Of course it's essential that our institutions stay financially afloat, and that they use credible and current financial strategies. I'm well aware that my paycheck depends on it. But there's more to educating than hawking a retail product. This is similar to household finances—my household is, in

5. Van Der Werf and Sabatier, *College of 2020*, 53.
6. Molloff, "*Waiting for Superman.*"
7. Lears, "Reform of the Reform," 24.

part, a business. We bring in money, spend money, keep the books, and forecast our financial future. If that's all we are, however, or even close to most of who we are, we're in deep trouble. Similarly, there's more to learning than consuming educational services. Again, in my home, we consume voraciously: meals, TV shows, clothes, tennis shoes, and bag after bag of Goldfish crackers. But all this consuming is a means to an end: the end is happy, energetic, purposeful living in our family and in our community. If consuming is all we are about, or even close to most of what we are about, we're in deep trouble. When allowed to self-direct, supply and demand become self-serving, totalizing forces that come to control the people and institutions they were supposed to serve. These forces need a *why*, a purpose defined, held, and maintained by people.

The business model suggests it is wrong, or selfish, for the teacher to put herself in the game as a whole-hearted participant in all that happens in class. It sounds high-minded to describe this as "student-centered," but this may be rationale for locking teachers and students into a patron-client dependency. The teacher is the service provider and the student is the consumer: they pay to receive a service, and we are paid to provide it. The consumer deserves the full measure of what she has paid for: it would be wrong for the Kwik-E-Mart clerk to take a sip of ICEE before handing it over, or for the customer to promise to pay Tuesday for a hamburger today. Such is life in market economies, or at least the public, cash-based part of life, which is rapaciously commodifying parts of life once seen as exempt from market logic, like human identity, bodies, faces, childhood, and teaching and learning.

Gift economies were the way of our human ancestors, and vestiges remain in the nonmarket dimensions of our lives, such as exchanging birthday gifts, sharing with neighbors, and living in a family.[8] Gifting involves obligations to give, receive, and repay. This is the glue of social solidarity in gift-based societies. The obligations of reciprocity link people together in life and beyond, as ancestors and spirits often also participate in gifting.

In his seminal work *The Gift*, sociologist Marcel Mauss concludes that there are no free gifts, "but in fact they are given and repaid under obligation."[9] There is no free gift, nor should there be, because a free gift either terminates relationship or creates dependency. Even in market economies, people recognize the power of the gift in nonmarket exchanges,

---

8. Mauss, *Gift*.

9. Ibid., 1.

such as birthday and holiday giving, or informal exchange networks among friends and neighbors. We often express pride and delight in sharing that benefits both parties and sometimes also society, but that doesn't involve paychecks, lawsuits, or dollar bills, such as child care collectives or neighborhood tool shares. It feels like getting one over on capitalism, because it is.

When teaching and learning are exchanged as gifts, they involve long-term relationships of obligation. The student mostly receives, often for many years, and is in turn obligated to repay not the teacher specifically, but society. The cost of an education should be very high, but not merely in dollars: it should invoke the honor, duty, and social responsibility of the student. Repayment is, by necessity, imprecise and ongoing: precise measure would terminate relationship and leave a graduate with the possibility of, say, going to Wall Street and doing whatever it takes to get rich, even if that means others in society will pay dearly for your wealth. Despite and often contrary to curriculum that encourages ethical citizenship, the medium by which this message is conveyed speaks louder: the logic of the business model implies that as long as you pay off your college loans, you don't owe anything to anybody.

In a gift economy, it is impossible to be only a giver, or only a taker. The teacher receives ongoing education, gaining depth of wisdom and character, through the practice of teaching. The teacher is obligated too, because she was once a student (and in a sense, always is). Serving as a teacher is repayment for all that previous generations invested in her. Because repayment is ongoing and never terminated, it's one of the deep social bonds that ties teachers to the society in which they serve. When gift economy and market economy function together, the teacher receives all he has truly earned: both paycheck and honor; cash and social recognition; monetary gain and the satisfaction of having contributed to society. When teaching is reduced to market logic, the teacher owes merely what the union or employer requires, and receives merely a paycheck. Money finds its fullest meaning in a context larger than itself, as a tool in a human economy that also values persons, virtues, and gifts; yet its seemingly unstoppable tendency is to become the context in which such things are valued and understood.

It is challenging, but not impossible, to keep gift economies alive during a time when markets are so voracious. We do it well in the private spheres of life, exchanging goods and services with imprecision and long time delays within families and friendships. When we treat education as more than a market transaction, even as we give the market what it is due, we remind our students that their education makes them responsible players on a field larger than their own personal lives—society, the human community, the global environment. We remind ourselves of that, too.

The next morning in Amsterdam, I had to face the students who had seen me undressing. I considered every way around it, my best options being to fake my own death or pay someone to kidnap me. But in college as at the circus, the show must go on. The five women who had seen me were sitting together, and when I walked toward the front of class, I caught their eyes and tugged at my shirt as if to emphasize the fact that I was fully clothed. They smiled, and one gave me a thumbs-up.

I made a personal vow to keep my clothes on when in the company of students and have kept it, with one exception. Several years after that class in Amsterdam, I became pregnant with twins. Thirty weeks along, I went to the obstetrician for a regular checkup. Nothing about this pregnancy had been regular, however: a litany of problems put both the babies and me at risk. The obstetrician saw signs of preterm labor and wheeled me straight to a hospital room to try to stop labor. She gave the babies a drug to hasten lung development in case they would be born, and another medication to prevent the progression of labor. I was terrified: at week thirty, the babies were likely to be born living, though there was no promise even of that, and could have major problems with brain, eye, or lung development. The magnesium sulfate made me disoriented and hot, hotter than I can ever remember being. A nurse took off my hospital gown and sheets and turned down the room temperature. My husband shivered in a sweatshirt and jacket while I laid there like a stuffed turkey in a pan, splayed and roasting.

In the middle of the night, a nurse woke me to check my vitals. She read my chart, then my face, and said, "Hey, Dr. Paris, it's Katie Olson. I was in your Intro to Anthropology class three years ago." Naked and sweating, flat on my back with a gigantic belly, I tried denial, "No, I'm not Dr. Paris." She smiled and stroked my arm. "Forget about it, Jenell. I'm going to do everything I can to help."

What a gift—my former student now played an important role in preserving my unborn children's lives. When I reflected on it later, I was glad to see that years after taking my class, she embodied the gist of Introduction to Cultural Anthropology: to see from multiple viewpoints (that I was her professor was only one view—more importantly, I was a pregnant woman in medical crisis), and to honor the needs of the vulnerable. I'm sure she learned these skills in nursing classes too, but I'd like to believe that my class made a difference in her life—that she came away a little more compassionate and empathetic.

Though she didn't have to, Katie kept checking in on my case during the thirty-three days between that crisis and the twins' healthy births. She visited me shortly after they were born and pronounced them beautiful.

Like pregnancy and childbirth, spiritual journeys are very personal, but not private. The quality of our inner lives—our ability to give and receive love, forgiveness, joy, and the rest—inevitably influences our students. The stakes are high and the challenges of the world are extreme: in addition to knowing about the world—quantifying, observing and studying it—our students, and we no less, need to learn to live well in it. The invitation is for teachers to *attend* their own classes, and to let students see us as we do.

3

Teach Here, Now

Geese appear high over us,
pass, and the sky closes. Abandon,
as in love or sleep, holds
them to their way, clear
in the ancient faith: what we need
is here. And we pray, not
for new earth or heaven, but to be
quiet in heart, and in eye,
clear. What we need is here.

—Wendell Berry, "The Wild Geese"

Most Sociology and Anthropology majors at my college study abroad, so I'm glad to give five or ten minutes of class time to recruiters from various international programs. A young man arrived at my Introduction to Cultural Anthropology class to pitch his Central America program. He enthused, "You've got to study abroad—get out there and change the world instead of just sitting in a classroom. Live life, don't just read about it in books!"

Enticed by the notion that I'd be better off elsewhere, I stammered through the first part of my lecture as the recruiter collected his materials before leaving. I worried he'd find my approach to "Subsistence Systems in Cross-Cultural Perspective" to be hopelessly out of touch with the world out there.

After class, I found a few colleagues I knew would be supportive and railed, "I opened my classroom to that guy, and he undermined everything we're doing there!" They agreed completely. A history professor declared, "Tell those students they could change the world if only they'd read their books!" After all, reading books slowly and entirely cultivates the kind of detailed, refined, and evidenced perspectives that students need if they're going to last as world-changers.

Truly, of course, classrooms and real-world education thrive in symbiosis. The classroom cultivates the long patience of scholarship, offering depth, critical thinking, and the wisdom gained from reading entire books. Study abroad programs do this to varying degrees, as well, but excel at setting students in unfamiliar contexts where new questions about the world and the self emerge from immersion and adventure. I'm tempted by every study abroad program I hear about. I want to see for myself the birds and insects of Belize, the rebuilding of Rwanda, the beaches of Samoa, and the architecture of Rome. I glean the fields of my students' experiences, poring over their photographs and handling their trinkets, amazed that they were really *there*.

For students, real life may seem to begin in the future, after high school, after college, after graduate school. Real life happens sometime other than *now*, and some place other than *here*. Adults chide students about what things are like in "the real world," which is somewhere other than where the student is at present. They say the same to us teachers, as if academic employment is something other than real. Teachers may peer over the fence at another discipline, another pedagogical style, or another location as the *there* where we could really be the teachers we were meant to be.

But once you arrive *there*, then you're *here*, and *there* begins to tantalize again from afar. Wendell Berry writes that quietness of heart and clarity of eye reveals that what we need is here. Seems true enough for geese in the sky, but for teachers in schools?

Here, nearly every year of my life, has been a classroom. At three, I was a student in my older sister's classroom, her bedroom, learning to write and read and above all else, to listen to the teacher, a kindergartener herself. I entered my first real classroom a few weeks after I turned five and admired my teacher with purity of heart. Miss Brilia was a fusion of angel, Wonder Woman, and Miss America, and I did everything I could to please her. I wanted to be her, a fantasy I would project on all my good teachers from kindergarten through graduate school.

I've lived on the academic calendar every year since then, taking no more than a summer's break between high school, college, graduate school, and working as a professor. I interpret the major events of my life with reference to the academic year, a yearly rhythm that marks time more truly than the calendar year. When I was a child, my family once moved across the country, just before school started. We visited Hawaii, our ultimate family vacation, during Spring Break. James and I scheduled our wedding around the demands of my doctoral fieldwork. Our youngest son was born during Spring Break, our twins at the beginning of a summer break. It would mean less to describe these events as having happened in June, April, or December.

Nonetheless, the worry that this isn't enough, neither for me nor for my students, often intrudes. Just sitting in *this* classroom, reading *these* books, with *this* teacher? The real deal must be somewhere else. In my first year of teaching, adrenaline and nerves would nearly make me sick before class, awash with excitement and terror. *I'm the professor? They're really letting me do this?* Now, nearly twenty years in, I hit different limits. I get frustrated by the constraints of budgets, class sizes, and institutional regulations, which easily expands into despair at my own constraints, realizing in this mid-career time that *this* is all I have to work with: this vita, this brain, this college, these students. It's tempting to imagine a more exotic location, a more recognizable discipline, smaller class sizes, or a lighter teaching load. The fantasy of being a smarter scholar, a more skilled teacher (or even just a more popular one) often allures.

That lecture on subsistence systems focused on the Ju/'hoansi, an indigenous group in the Kalahari Desert of Botswana and Namibia. They're unusually famous by hunter-gatherer standards, having hosted many journalists, travel writers, and anthropologists, and they became known to the broader world for their starring role in *The Gods Must Be Crazy* films. In the early 1950s, Harvard University sent an expedition to explore the region and see whether these fabled people were really there, perhaps in a lost city. The explorers drove for weeks without seeing a road, a person, or any human development. The city never emerged, but the Ju/'hoansi did (then called !Kung, Bushmen, or San). To outsiders, their land seems mostly flat, barren, and dry. The Ju/'hoansi, however, knew their environment so intimately that they could easily find over ninety varieties of plants and water-bearing roots. Their hunting skills were awe-inspiring: not only could they identify animals by their tracks, they could analyze footprints and droppings to assess how recently the animal passed by, where it was likely headed, and how its health or injuries would influence its course. They prized mobility and freedom over accumulation, and stored very little. One anthropologist said that for hunter-gatherers, nature is God's refrigerator: what they need is there.

I show a black-and-white photo of 1950's Ju/'hoansi women gathering mongongo nuts to a third grade class. I'm giving a career talk about "What Professors Do." The women in the photograph wear simple coverings and karosses (gathering implements), several with babies tied to their backs. Naked toddlers play nearby.

I ask the students, "What do you see?"

"Poor people."

"Those women look hungry."

"Those kids have no clothes."

They got it right, at first glance and from a first world perspective, but anthropologists see it differently. The women in that photograph, and their male counterparts, worked about twenty hours a week to get the food they needed to survive. Everyone was dressed appropriately, by their own standards. Anthropologist Marshall Sahlins posited that their way of life was, in fact, original affluence, the heritage of our species. "There may be two possible courses to affluence. Wants may be 'easily satisfied' either by producing much or desiring little."[1] In other words, the experience of wealth may be achieved by having more, or by wanting less. In what they had, and in what they longed for, the Ju/'hoansi enjoyed abundance. They had plentiful food, adequate water, and enjoyment of family and leisure.

Over thousands of years, they continually adapted to a remote desert environment and it yielded abundance. At present they are under tremendous stress as globalization has hit them full force, introducing social inequality and material goods previously unknown, resulting in violence, alcohol abuse, militarization, and low-wage labor. Though they have lost

---

1. Sahlins, *Stone Age Economics*, 2.

members to all these intrusions, their population is strong and growing. As a small, unarmed, decentralized and remote people, Ju/'hoansi survived for centuries by taking a flexible and amenable attitude toward outsiders and toward change. Today they are multicultural, multilingual, and skilled in multiple modes of subsistence (hunting and gathering, working for cash, agriculture, and ecotourism). They collaborate with anthropologists and others to improve health care, literacy, and language and culture transmission. At times they mobilize for collective action to change political and economic systems, but more often they adapt to daily circumstances. Many also live in settlement squalor and dependency on foreign aid.

Their current environment is far from just, adequate, or respectful of their traditions and culture. Nonetheless, they continue to display the strength of the foraging way of life, with clever adaptation to circumstances. They do what they can within their own limits, and the limits of their environment.

I lecture to my college students about adaptation, that amazing human capacity to shift, flex, and manage new environments very quickly and often, very effectively. Students discuss:

- *How did Ju/'hoansi adapt to their early twentieth-century environment?*
- *How are they adapting to globalization?*
- *In both time periods, do you notice any elements that could be labeled maladaptive?*
- *By what criteria would you measure adaptation or maladaptation?*

Culture is both window and mirror, says a well-used catchphrase of anthropologists everywhere. After looking through the window at an extremely different culture, we turn to the mirror.

- *How does our way of life represent an adaptation to circumstances?*
- *What elements could be labeled maladaptive, and why?*

Studying extremely different cultural Others can be merely an exercise in ethnocentrism, misunderstanding the Other by viewing them from the vantage point of the self. Or it can be reverse ethnocentrism, berating ourselves for losing what to our eye seems the "simple life," focused on relationships and in touch with nature and with things that really matter. If we can avoid these pitfalls, we can see both Others and ourselves, wherever is *here* for us and for them, with both critique and compassion.

Though the details vary in substance and severity, *here* always has limitations, whether for indigenous people adapting to globalization, or for teachers adapting to new challenges in their profession. Many of these challenges, for us and for them, come from the pressures of global capitalism shaping time, law, relationships, material things, and communication. We are both pushed toward change and enticed by new possibilities, and the combined force of push and pull is impossible to resist.

Our problems are surely "First World problems," but they mirror, and are linked to, problems everywhere on the globe. Our classrooms, our own abilities, and certainly the broader context of education in the early twenty-first century, are far from pristine, perfect, or even adequate. All is not well here, but *here* is what we've got. As Wendell Berry writes, geese fly with abandon: could we teach the same way?

Our practice begins here, now, as things are. Buddhist teacher Karen Maezen Miller writes, "Your life is your practice. Your spiritual practice does not occur someplace other than in your life right now, and your life is nowhere other than where you are. You are looking for answers, insight, and wisdom that you already possess. Live the life in front of you, be the life you are, and see what you find out for yourself."[2]

[T]eaching has the potential to become spiritual practice when we encounter within our own depths our fears and desires, our real relation to our students and subjects, and the sacred in and among us.

—MARIA LICHTMANN[3]

When I started college, there were plenty of reasons for fear: college costs were starting to creep upward, AIDS was still spreading and poorly understood, maps were being redrawn with the fall of economic communism. Global problems were not easily engaged or even understood, and I carried the weight of the world on my young, studious, and ethically rigid

---

2. Miller, *Momma Zen*, 6.
3. Lichtmann, *Teacher's Way*, 33.

shoulders. Imagine my surprise when a highly esteemed professor started rapping his way through fourth-century Rome. *Augustine was born in 3–5–4 / his mother was a Christian but his daddy swore.* Dr. Turner wore his academic regalia and bounded back and forth across the width of the classroom, trying to enunciate clearly enough for us to take notes without compromising the rhythm and bounce of his white middle-aged rapping. I felt embarrassed for him, the shame a teenager bears on behalf of her unredeemable parents, but then realized I didn't need to. A friend leaned over and said, "Wow, he is super into this!" Students laughed, watched, and took notes, all at the same time.

Mr. Jacobs' fourth-grade class was the pinnacle of elementary school. He gave a test on state capitols that was anticipated for years with lunchroom and school bus rumors that inflated the challenge to epic proportions. When students passed, he praised us as if we had climbed a mountain.

My kids' kindergarten teacher wrote a reading and counting curriculum based on poetry. I'd never seen Shel Silverstein's "Hug-o-War" taught with such zeal.

In a community education class, not only did I learn how to macramé lawn chairs, I was transported into a zone of timelessness and pure focus by a teacher whose driving passion was restoration of old lawn chairs.

These teachers taught with abandon: wholeheartedness in the face of their own limits, and those of their schools and world. Rather than losing themselves in anxiety, anger, doubt, or frustration over limits—be they personal, political, or other kinds—they lost themselves in the act of teaching which is, of course, the best way for a teacher to really find himself.

Teaching is our necessity and the classroom is our environment. A classroom full of students may sometimes seem like barren land, but with agility and insight, it can yield spiritual abundance for the professor. A rapidly changing professional environment, hit by global changes that no one is controlling or directing, can seem like an impossible limit, but with daily adaptations, and mobilization or collective action when possible, it's possible to do more than merely acquiesce. Responding to flaws with cutting critique, avoidance, or ineffectual complaint are all varieties of hot anger which, even if originating in just cause, pours fuel on the fire. As mystic Eckhart Tolle observes, "Acceptance of the unacceptable is the greatest source of grace in this world."[4] It is possible to approach flaws and limits—in our students, our educational systems, and of course, our own selves—with

---

4. Tolle, *Stillness Speaks*, 71.

the wisdom and grace of acceptance, which is not acquiescence. Instead, it is grace that liberates us from our desire to control, direct, or even fully understand the teaching life. We are free to indulge the humor, intensity, skill, and passion that come when we let go.

All is not well here, but here we are, so here is where we practice. Abandon may be inevitable, over time, but we can choose its direction. We can choose to give ourselves over to teaching as a financial necessity—*I need this job, and I've sunk so many years into the system, I can't choose another*—or we can hold on to the higher hope that teaching is one of our spiritual necessities, a practice that makes our hearts full and whole.

The invitation is to teach with abandon, here, now, as we are. This will hold us to the way. It need not involve rapping, unless that's your thing.

4

Have Fun

The intelligence can only be led by desire. For there to be desire, there must be pleasure and joy in the work. The intelligence only grows and bears fruit in joy. The joy of learning is as indispensable in study as breathing is in running. Where it is lacking there are no real students, but only poor caricatures of apprentices who, at the end of their apprenticeship, will not even have a trade.

—Simone Weil, *Waiting for God*

I once taught a teacher development seminar titled "Teaching Just for Fun." There's more to my classes, I explained, than the course objectives that align with general education requirements and college mission, and that are delineated according to the college handbook. There is always one more objective: to have fun.

I even set up classroom activities for my own amusement. "Trust me," I tell students, "the more fun I have, the more you'll learn." Theory Throwdown, for example, is a game in which students compete to persuade a three-judge panel of their peers that one social theory is best. "There's a prize," I say, which makes them try hard. The game is funny enough, as students endorse sociobiology, symbolic interactionism, or structural-functionalism as if their lives depend on it. At the end, the prize turns out to be prestige, a valuable social reward that we symbolize with applause. We laugh: class dismissed.

In the teacher development seminar, we took two minutes of silence to reflect:

Remember a time when you had fun teaching—when you were totally engaged and really alive, experiencing joy, pleasure, and focus. Dwell on the details.

A biology teacher responded, "When we do wild stuff like going outside and getting our hands dirty."

A math teacher said, "Experiencing the euphoria of a mathematical proof, and seeing the students get it."

A psychology teacher recalled, "I set up a new small group system, and when I saw it working, it made me happy."

We talked about going into the new semester looking for pleasure, indulging our delight in teaching, and trusting that teaching "just for fun" will be good for students. A communication professor said, "Wow, it feels so good to be given permission to enjoy myself."

... professors must practice being vulnerable in the classroom, being wholly present in mind, body, and spirit.

—BELL HOOKS[1]

Now, I don't mean the supposed pleasure of monologuing before a captive audience about a topic of interest only to you. Examples abound, but the one that comes to mind is Dr. Frame, self-professed "prophet of doom," who held forth three hours at a time on only one topic, Marxist critique of global capitalism. He said he didn't believe in class discussion: we students needed to listen and take notes, not opine about what we hadn't yet learned. He seemed to enjoy listening to himself talk, but I don't think it was truly enjoyable for him or for us. A well-delivered lecture certainly can be pleasurable, but in a way similar to a musical performance. I know a music professor and pianist who is always seeking an audience. He says, "It just isn't the same without an audience. I need them." He draws himself and his listeners into a shared encounter with the music. Whether music

---

1. hooks, *Teaching to Transgress*, 21.

performance or lecturing, it's obvious when people are actively listening, and when they are biding their time. It's equally obvious when teachers are educating and inspiring, and when they are just holding forth.

The teachers in my seminar linked their pleasure to student engagement: getting *our* hands dirty, figuring out a proof *and seeing students get it*. No one said they loved assessment, standardization, objectives, or goals: words like *joy, pleasure,* and *happy* were reserved for things like "a-ha" moments of understanding, using hands and feet and noses to explore the subject, and being caught up—students and teacher together—in learning. Standardized experiences and objective measures may be required of us, but we dare not settle for so little; delight comes from engaging the wildness, the beauty, the chaos, and the order of reality itself. Theatre teacher Rachel Shteir explains, "I try to teach students how to experience pleasure reading great works of literature and seeing great works of art. . . . I try to teach them about the timeless, the universal, and what the dramaturg Mark Bly calls 'the questioning spirit.'" Schools should, in Shteir's words, "create an oasis for inquiry," not merely hold audiences captive for ever-talking heads.[2]

The practice is to have fun teaching, to pursue pleasure, joy, happiness, and delight. Buddhist teacher Thich Nhat Hanh offers a poem for recitation during meditation:

> Breathing in, I calm my body.
> Breathing out, I smile.
> Dwelling in the present moment
> I know this is a beautiful moment.[3]

This meditation is hardly complicated—just breathe. Pleasure can be even more simple. Just smile. Just laugh. Just have fun. For critical thinkers, however, this may not seem simple at all. Smiling, delighting, resting, and enjoying can seem like bourgeois luxuries that ignore or magnify the suffering of the proletariat (I still have my notes from Dr. Frame's class). Happiness can seem simple-minded and unsophisticated, precritical, nontheoretical, and nonanalytical. Joy in learning is necessary perhaps for kindergarteners, but not for more serious students. Happiness, joy, and

---

2. Shteir, "MOOCs and the Arts."
3. Hanh and Ellsberg, *Thich Nhat Hanh,* 25.

pleasure probably aren't in the assessment rubric, or listed among the objectives to be mastered before the standardized tests.

A smile may not be sophisticated and critical, but it is important. Hanh explains, "Every day we touch what is wrong, and, as a result, we are becoming less and less healthy. That is why we have to learn to practice touching what is not wrong—inside us and around us. When we get in touch with our eyes, our heart, our liver, our breathing, and our non-toothache and really enjoy them, we see that the conditions for peace and happiness are already present."[4]

Every other year at my college, students and faculty host a public science event. At the Physics vs. Chemistry showdown, they compete for audience applause by starting minor fires and explosions, freezing flowers in liquid nitrogen and throwing them against a wall (they shatter), making "elephant toothpaste" with a chemical reaction that makes huge quantities of foam, channeling static electricity to make hair stand on end, and so on. For me, the best thing about the event is the childlike enthusiasm of the professors. The glee on Dr. Smith's face is that of a little boy starting fires and making things explode. *Look what I can do! Now check this out! And this!* Students and professors alike clamor for audience attention, urging everyone to see how cool science can be.

I know these scientists, students and faculty both, struggle with the difficulty of their subjects. I hear of their strenuous homework and research projects, and I admire their important applications to health care, infrastructure, and the environment. "Elephant toothpaste" is important too, however, because it keeps them in touch with what is not wrong, what is not a problem, what is not a pressing crisis. Hanh elaborates, "Life is filled with suffering, but it is also filled with many wonders, like the blue sky, the sunshine, the eyes of a baby. To suffer is not enough. We must also be in touch with the wonders of life. They are within us and all around us, everywhere, any time."[5]

A snowstorm made me lose touch with all that is not wrong. I worried my way through a Tuesday afternoon class, one eye on the falling snow and one on my notes. *This is too much snow. I should cancel so commuters can get home safely. But if we don't get through this material, we'll be behind for weeks. And besides, I'm not supposed to cancel without a college*

4. Ibid., 23.
5. Ibid., 24.

announcement. I indulged my worries by ending class one minute early, at 5:14. I headed straight home, a half-mile commute that normally takes ninety seconds, arriving with a migraine and tears in my eyes at 6:00. Wednesday and Thursday classes were cancelled, unprecedented double snow days due to back-to-back blizzards that dumped a total of three feet of snow in our valley.

Massive amounts of snow come rarely in South Central Pennsylvania, and students responded like shoppers headed to Walmart on Black Friday, streaming toward Cemetery Hill from the dorms. Cemetery Hill is, surprisingly enough, a lively campus spot. A cemetery rests at the top of a wide, steep hill that gives way to an expanse of flat ground below. Students brought the most slippery thing they possessed: sleds, cafeteria trays, cardboard boxes, or just their own backsides.

My boys begged to go sledding. With them at ages four, four, and two, I knew I couldn't keep all three of them safe on my own. I invited some students to come out and play with us, and Nicolena agreed to meet us at the hill.

I arrived first and stood at the bottom, wary. I grew up in Minnesota so I know my way around a sledding hill, and this was a dangerous one. The snow fell so quickly on the relatively warm ground that the bottom layer turned to ice. The snow on top was heavy and water-logged, so sleds, canoes, and undergraduate backsides packed it down into ice on top of ice. Even more dangerous than the hill was the traffic pattern of sledders. When hills are used regularly for sledding, decorum emerges. People respect established pathways for trudging up the hill, and they steer clear of the bottom where sledders are careening out of control. This scene, however, was mayhem. People scrambling up the hill were being hit by those whizzing down, and groups congregated at the foot of the hill, jumping out of the way when a sled was about to hit them. Through their hats and hoods, my boys barely heard me over the noise of screaming sledders, "Don't go up the hill! We have to wait for Nicolena!"

A few minutes later we saw her walking over from the dorms, delicately picking her way through waist-high snow. She wore mismatched outdoor gear and, instead of snow boots, dress boots with slick bottoms. She broke her concentration to greet us with a smile, "Do you think these clothes will work? I had to borrow them. I've never sledded before."

"Sledding is easy," I said to Nicolena, "Just go up the hill and then slide down. Let's try to stay together."

Oliver and Wesley, the twins, raced up the hill, both dropping their sleds as they concentrated on climbing. Their riderless sleds made a beeline for the bottom of the hill. When I started back for the sleds, Max, my little one, pitched a fit. "I'm scared!" He tried to run away from me up the hill, but just slipped in place on the ice. I snatched him out of the way of an oncoming sled and shouted to Nicolena, "Go down and get the twins' sleds and come back up!" She tried, but couldn't hold all the sleds and maneuver up the hill in her slippery boots, especially while laughing so hard. I got over to her and managed to hold all four sleds in one arm and Max in the other, but I couldn't get up the hill, either. Tired of waiting, Oliver and Wesley came down and got their sleds and, with no fear or concern for safety, hurled themselves down the slope. Nicolena half-rolled, half-slid down the hill with no sled at all.

I stayed at the bottom with my toddler while Nicolena and the twins found their rhythm, the boys doing daredevil runs down the hill from as high a point as they could reach, and she cascading from a lower point, with or without a sled, meeting them at the bottom. They'd run over to me, the twins raving about the run as if I hadn't been standing there watching it. They'd race back up the hill, and Nicolena would attempt another ascent, ice-crusted mittens clawing, fashion boot toes stabbing the ground like faulty crampons.

A student ran past us, calling out to someone further on. "Dude! Look at my face!" It was red-cheeked, littered with bits of snow, with blood pouring from his mouth. He seemed elated.

Sledding lasted forty-five minutes or so, and then cold little fingers, ears, and noses needed to go home. Nicolena had walked less than a block from her dorm to the hill, but she agreed to let me drive her home. Cars and vans were parked helter-skelter at the foot of Cemetery Hill, and I had to back in and out of a driveway to get headed in the right direction. My minivan got stuck, front wheels spinning in a pit of ice and slush. "Shit!" I exclaimed, paused, then banged the steering wheel with both fists, "Shit!" My children fell silent, and so did Nicolena. *Shit! Not only did I swear in front of a student and my children, I paused and then did it again!* I told Nicolena to try pushing the van while I rocked it forward and reverse, but nothing worked. *Shit! I just asked a student to push my minivan!* This failed, so I resigned myself to living out of the van on the edge of campus until the snow melted.

While I began taking inventory of survival items (I had a day's supply of diapers, band-aids, and animal crackers), a man appeared. He seemed to have materialized out of the snow bank. He was very thin, and wore gloves and a hat but no coat, just layers of baggy earth-toned clothing and huge boots. His hair was long and shaggy and he had a beard. He scooped slush and ice from the pit until ground was visible. He waved over a few more drivers who, with me and Nicolena, rocked the van while he alternated forward and reverse acceleration. The van was freed, and my boys cheered. The man nodded to them silently, then headed off, disappearing down into the railroad track bed that runs past campus.

"Wow," I said to Nicolena, "that was cool."

"Yeah, that's Tyler Miller. He's a senior. He's really into the environment." Then she surveyed the entire situation and smiled. "This was fun."

"It was super fun," I said. "Sorry for swearing."

Several years before this, I taught a class that turned freezing cold, and not in a winter wonderland kind of way. Sex, Gender, and Culture got off to a good start. With only twenty students, all juniors and seniors, I was able to quickly learn their names and encourage them toward the kind of text-based discussion and student leadership that they would encounter in graduate school. After about four weeks, however, the class climate turned. Students avoided eye contact with me, stopped initiating discussion, and departed right after class instead of lingering to talk with me. It wasn't every single student, but it felt like it: a critical mass tipped the class ethos toward negativity. It seemed like a stalemate, but I didn't remember a conflict having begun.

I tried barreling on with techniques that had worked in earlier weeks, to no avail. I tried humor, and it fell flat. I resorted to lecturing just to avoid the awkward silences and downturned eyes that came in response to "What did you think of today's reading?"

Frustrated, I called my friend Margot, a professor expert in human well-being. "What's gone wrong?" I worried. "How am I going to get through this class? How are they going to make it through the rest of the semester?"

Margot agreed that my class was in a bad place. My approaches to fixing the problem, she observed, involved asserting more and more control. Perhaps I could try ceding control; not giving over to student negativity, but listening to concerns and responding to them. Though the official subject of the class was sex and gender, she wondered whether a deeper subject might be emerging: community and conflict. "I take you seriously as intellectuals," I had said on the first day of class. "If you live in the freedom that's here for you, we can make a learning community that is sharp and productive, and also gracious and loving." The class moved quickly toward this opportunity, with students taking chances, trying on ideas and then changing them, and helping each other understand difficult material. By the second week of the semester, it seemed, community was achieved.

M. Scott Peck explains that this honeymoon stage of community is actually pseudocommunity, an illusion instead of the real thing. Only after groups face conflict, chaos, and emptiness—deep threats to the viability of the group—can they progress toward genuine community that acknowledges and even anticipates difference and conflict, and forges pathways to reconciliation.[6]

Margot offered to come to class as a facilitator. She would lead a discussion about their grievances with the class and/or with me, summarize their responses for me, and then I would respond. This seemed drastic. I had never before (and never have since) given over my class to another professor because I couldn't handle it. I was afraid of what students might say about me, and that I'd lose my credibility with them. I was afraid Margot would think I was a terrible professor. But my distress over the class and my trust in my friend outweighed my concerns, so went for it.

The students told Margot about a time when a student made a comment, and I responded, "No, that isn't what the author meant . . . " and corrected the student without any affirmation of her attempt. When students were speaking, they said, I just stared at them, expressionless. And in general, I didn't smile very often. The student offended by my correction and her friends agreed that I didn't like them or their ideas, and my unsmiling face confirmed it. A few others joined these secessionists, and there we were, a class with nearly half its members unhappy.

I began to help us climb out of this pit by summarizing M. Scott Peck's stages of community. "In my view," I said, "this is a great opportunity. We can press through chaos and emptiness and move toward real community. But first things first, your professor's face." I explained that when I'm really interested in what someone is saying, I am so focused on the ideas that I don't think about my appearance. My intense attention, discussion of ideas, and correction of student perspectives are signs of affirmation and

6. Peck, *Different Drum*.

care, not anger or disregard. Seeing as it was a gender studies class, I wondered aloud whether students would respond similarly to a male professor with the same traits. Social expectations for females to be nurturing and concerned about their appearance are strong, and it can be jolting when a woman doesn't meet those expectations. I said I'd work on acknowledging the value of student contributions, if they would agree to learn how to learn from me as I am, not compare me to a smiling, nurturing stereotype of a woman. I offered a simple apology to the student whose feelings I had hurt. "When you're wrong, you're wrong," I said, "but I could have affirmed the sincerity of your effort, or linked your incorrect statement back to some other accurate comment you had made. I'll work on that."

Throughout, I worried about class descending into a waste of time, all process and no content. What about the actual content of the class: sex, gender, and culture? All in all, conflict resolution took about ninety minutes of class time, and it was worth every one. We shared a framework for the development of community that helped us anticipate and accept conflict, a valuable life lesson. We returned to course material with new efficiency, energy no longer drained by grievances. It became fun; after all, the conflict itself was laden with sex, gender, and culture—men and women in conflict with each other, in different power positions within an educational culture. It was a little like sledding down Cemetery Hill, exhilarating to career between disaster and delight.

Simone Weil says it well: "The intelligence can only be led by desire. For there to be desire, there must be pleasure and joy in the work. The intelligence only grows and bears fruit in joy." In Sex, Gender, and Culture, the desire was to correct course, and the joy was the deep satisfaction of working through conflict together.

The practice is pleasure, teaching just for fun. When pleasure and joy are embedded in the work of both students and teacher, the intelligence grows and bears fruit. Joy calls forth the spirits of the material, the students, and the teacher. In other words, people learn. In fact, that's precisely what wasn't fun about Dr. Frame's three-hour monologues. His ideas about justice and equality were moving and important, but he offered them with no vulnerability, humor, or delight; the kind of humanity necessary, in fact, to budge the world a little toward his collectivist utopia.

The day after sledding, I got to class a few minutes early and overheard Nicolena telling classmates about playing with my kids. Students rushed to recount their most dangerous runs and their most outrageous sledding devices (canoes, and an overturned banquet table).

I asked, "Did anyone see the guy who was running around bragging about the blood pouring out of his mouth?"

A couple of students laughed, "Yeah, we saw him."

One offered, "I know him. He had to go to health services, but he's OK now."

5

Say Yes, Say No

It occurs to me that exhorting my fellow teachers to take risks every day, to head for the artistic edge, might be enough to do us all in. Prepare your classes; teach school; read student papers; make helpful comments on them; keep office hours; meet with committees; spend quality time with your friends, children, and partners; cut your fat intake; practice meditation; get in your aerobic exercise; and, oh, in your spare time, be a visionary . . . .

—Mary Rose O'Reilley, *Radical Presence*

All you need to say is simply "Yes" or "No"; anything beyond this comes from the evil one.

—Matt 5:37, NIV

"We need five more people, and then the committee will be complete," the chair stated.

The committee was comprised of more than a dozen faculty members tasked with reviewing and revising a major portion of the college's curriculum. It would meet for two hours every two weeks for at least two years. I succumbed to the peer nomination and public flattery process that had occurred at an earlier faculty meeting. Others knew better: even being buttered up before an audience of one's peers did not persuade enough people to fill the required number of slots.

"Maybe we should ask Helen," someone suggested.

"Don't bother," came a reply, "she says no to things."

While many unemployed teachers wish they had jobs, the flip side of that coin is that those of us left standing in education have more work than we can possibly do. At small teaching colleges, in addition to teaching six or eight or ten classes each year, a faculty member may be officially required to serve on a few committees, but in reality, many do five, six, or seven. There may be one committee whose work you are truly devoted to, but another requires a representative from your department, another needs gender, racial, or ethnic balance, the president appointed you to one, and your dean implored you not to drop off the other. The other three are ad hoc, so they shouldn't last more than a year or two. Then there's academic advising, mentoring students, advising student groups, making bulletin boards for your department hallway, and so on. This is part of what biology professor Nichole McDaniel calls "shadow workload," the parts of a teacher's job "that can't really be defined."[1]

In a painfully titled article, "No Time to Think," David M. Levy laments how "the acceleration and overloading of academic life" squeezes out time for what used to be considered central pursuits: thinking, considering, and reflecting.[2] Heather Menzies considers workplace changes across industries including health care and education: running short-staffed and under-resourced is the new norm; technology constantly changes, and in multiple domains; the Internet has created pressure to work and be available 24–7; individual etiquette and organizational norms for this new environment have not yet stabilized. The collective effects are costly: "a social environment being rendered toxic by an inhuman pace and dangerously irresponsible by an abstracted, disembodied form of presence."[3] Individual effects vary with workplace, but for many teachers, we work in a frenzy of keeping up with emails, working with inadequate resources, and meeting increasingly complex, laborious, and nonsensical standards of extremely

1. June, "Budget Cuts."
2. Levy, "No Time to Think," 238.
3. Menzies, *No Time*, 61.

distant regulators. Menzies fears that teachers are "losing what has been a taken-for-granted rootedness in the rhythm and rituals of shared time and space. At some point perhaps we find surrogates in multitasking rituals and the frenzied rhythms of work."[4]

Early in my career, I ate lunch in the faculty lounge nearly every day. Anytime between 10:30 AM and 2:00 PM, I could count on finding at least three or four other faculty members there. We'd joke and chat, but also talk about things like the origins of Sanskrit, how to handle a difficult student situation, distinctions between subfields of history, and how to navigate the promotion and tenure system. This bond of professional fellowship influenced our advising, our teaching, and our faculty meetings. Today, the faculty lounge is almost always empty. For a while, I ate there alone, hoping my presence would magically call others to join me. Then I picked a lunch time and invited about fifteen colleagues to join me. "I eat in my office so I can keep doing email," one said. "How do you have the time?" another marveled. I've insisted that eating with colleagues is not a luxury; both the food and the collegiality fuel me for my work, which I do more efficiently and happily for having spent time with my scholarly community. We now fill a very small table on a regular basis, which seems a success, but it also seems there is no going back to the past where there were no invitations and no schedule; lunch just happened.

The fear is that we can't keep up—there's just too much to do. From K–12 to college, it seems, workload has increased while resources have dwindled. This fear is very real, and, depending on a teacher's temperament and power position within a school, we may respond by overworking, complaining, avoiding, or offering half-hearted efforts. Letting love cast out this fear is easier said than done.

Professors who embrace the challenge of self-actualization will be better able to create pedagogical practices that engage students, providing them with ways of knowing that enhance their capacity to live fully and deeply.

—BELL HOOKS[5]

---

4. Ibid., 85.

5. hooks, *Teaching to Transgress*, 22.

I was impressed and intrigued by Helen's reputation. I looked at my load of committees, taskforces, working groups, independent studies, informal faculty advisement and sponsorship of student activities, and worried that instead of being the sacrificial giver I imagined myself to be, I was just gaining a reputation for being someone who says yes to things. I didn't want to someday look back at my career and see a junkyard of writing and research; once-valuable ventures, half-completed or forgotten, that I hadn't tended or arranged. I didn't want to say "yes," and then only put in half-hearted effort such as irregular meeting attendance or rubber-stamping decisions. I wanted boundaries, or limits, on my job, but I didn't know where to draw those lines. One thing that did seem clear was that no one else was going to draw them for me.

Certain parts of Helen's life seemed avidly untended. She shared her love of nature with everyone by refusing to use deodorant. Months after some imported cheese was finally consumed or removed, her car emanated a stinky cheese/wet dog aroma (she also had a huge dog that often accompanied her). On a camping trip with colleagues, she drove us past the last gas station into the wilderness, gas gauge alert flashing, with a laugh, "It's not serious when it says that. It'll go sixty more miles."

In other respects, however, she seemed like a woman with a plan. Tenured faculty are reputed to say "no" to lots of things in favor of doing nothing. As a teaching assistant, I saw this firsthand. I used to turn on videos in a class for a professor who said he just didn't want to walk up the stairs to the classroom. Helen's "no" was different than this: it stood guard for her "yes." She met institutional expectations for committee-sitting and faculty meeting-attending, and others in her small department valued her contributions. She went above and beyond, joining students in their activist campaigns, taking them camping, and bringing students and faculty together for meals and conversation at her home.

Instead of such happy industriousness, teachers often live under the tyranny of the urgent. Bullied by institutional needs and shrinking resources, we open out our pants pockets and watch our treasured time and energy disappear. It seems there's no choice: the work and its importance seem to be fixed, and our willingness to do it is the only variable. In some respects, this is true—next year's contract, promotion, or tenure do, in fact, hang on performance.

This produces a temptation (for me, an often irresistible one) to treat the moments and years of a teaching career as means to an end. Dynamics vary across educational settings, but our common context of rapid technological change and economic contraction produces similar pressures. For example, in pursuing a scholarly career, graduate school is, in large part, a means to an end. Most professors devote seven to ten years to the process. I worked long hours, dissolved boundaries between work and home, and devoted both personal and professional energy to earning my doctorate in hopes that it would lead to a faculty position in which I could be settled. Securing a tenure-track assistant professorship carried similar pressures: overwork for the sake of promotion and tenure, a process that would take the better part of a decade, if not longer. And once completed, at the full professor rank with tenure, urgency about meeting institutional needs continues, the pressure flowing less from promotion and tenure concerns and more from commitment to relationships and systems I've come to value.

Eventually the committee was assembled and its work proceeded. After months of unproductive two-hour meetings every two weeks, I appealed for release from my obligation.

The committee chair asked, "Do you have any hobbies, like doodling or knitting?"

I started crocheting during meetings as a way to pass the time but maintain my presence. Six more months and four baby sweaters later, I began to obsess—only during meetings—about my eventual demise: whether next week or in fifty years, I would, on my deathbed, regret the hours I'd sat on this committee. I resigned. Many moons later, the committee finished its work and presented it to the college faculty who voted it down.

Several years later I moved to a new college and paid my dues with a hodgepodge of new courses ranging from Women's Studies to Religious History to Freshman Writing to Contemporary Issues in a field other than the one in which I earned my doctorate, and advising, and committees. When I'd review the pile of uncompleted work remaining on a Friday afternoon, I could hardly remember how it got there, much less how I'd get it done. I felt hurt and powerless, and insisted that people and processes beyond my control were forcing me to overwork. I would cry on the drive home from work as evening migraines began, shooting lightning bolts across my eyes or creating what looked like blue goggles in my line of sight. I'd struggle to get my three little boys to bed, and then return to the computer to return emails or prep the next class. Sometimes before bed I'd slip into Wesley's room and lay down beside his warm three-year-old body. I'd put my hand on his chest and try to relax to the beating of his heart.

But I needed more than comfort: I needed a change. More imminent than my eventual deathbed regret over committee service, I feared watching my boys race off to kindergarten, having missed the clear happiness of these years because I'd seen their preschool selves through blue-goggled migraines.

I pored over Mary Rose O'Reilley's *The Garden at Night: Burnout and Breakdown in the Teaching Life,* in which she uses koans to interpret the difficulties of academic life. A koan is like an unanswerable riddle, a question such as "What is the sound of one hand clapping?" or "What was your face before you were born?" The purpose of meditating on a koan is to knock the brain off the tracks it habitually rides, opening up space for new wisdom and perspective. I found my own professional koan and carried it for a year: *why have I taught ten new preps in two years?*

Allow some space and silence in your classroom and watch how everything changes—everything is up for grabs, your whole life. If you really look at your day, the dislocations become apparent. Fortunately, in this quiet space, you can also learn what you need to do to survive.

—Mary Rose O'Reilley[6]

My husband wondered whether I, he, and most everyone else live like addicts, compulsively reaching for things that don't bring contentment. Instead of changing course, we just keep doing the same thing. I once heard a colleague rejoice at being appointed to a committee, "I finally feel needed!" I realized that was key to understanding his workplace behavior: he thrived when he felt people needed him, and when they didn't, he would construct problems or crises in order to be the one who resolved them. Being indispensable is not my drug of choice; rather, it's goodness. I want to be good, to do good, and to be affirmed by others, especially superiors, as having done good. Others may crave success, or the emotional high that comes from frenzied fatigue, or the chance to amass enough power to have influence. We are hooked on being busy, being admired, or achieving prestige or perfection. We satisfy these cravings daily, in the way we teach and the way

6. O'Reilley, *Garden at Night*, xiv.

we serve our institutions, but once indulged, the high is temporary and, at some level, disappointing.

The spiritual challenge is to simply say "yes" or "no," not to give ourselves away, or refuse to give anything at all, in order to satisfy an addiction. Discernment means learning to do the right thing for the right reason. This may mean saying "no" when someone else could do the job, or when you have another priority that deserves to be protected. It might mean coming to terms with a genuine "yes" that is grounded in obligation, when the work simply has to be done, or because your refusal would be refused.

I hung a copy of the Serenity Prayer in our kitchen.

> God grant me the grace to accept the things I cannot change,
> the courage to change the things I can,
> and the wisdom to know the difference.

I was doing the inverse; resisting the things I couldn't change (some of my course assignments, for instance), doing little to change the things I could (some of my course assignments, for instance), and having no sense of which was which.

Eventually the koan worked its magic. I perceived choices where there had seemed to be none. In an anthropology class, a student commented on women's empowerment among the Waorani, an indigenous horticulturalist society in the Amazon rainforest. Before they were drawn into the global system, Waorani lived effectively and pragmatically, with a minimal sexual division of labor. Men and women alike were expected to strike the right balance between self-sufficiency and interdependence. Sarah, an undergraduate, said, "I'd like to act more like that. I mean, we have lots of freedom, but we don't necessarily act like it. Waorani women have power, and they act like they do."

In one sense, it's true that my choices are limited, but they aren't as limited as when I worked as a steakhouse waitress. I learned that job by watching a corporate video, and my task was to do the work as prescribed. I was trained, not educated. I was paid for performing a task, not embodying a role. I was not to reinterpret the task, personalize it, or work on it at home. I realized I was squeezing a professor job into the mold of a restaurant server. For many faculty, course assignments, committees, and informal obligations are negotiated, at least some of the time and to some degree, and almost always across power differences, structural or interpersonal.

I asked myself, *Why do I say yes when I want to say no? Why do I bear the urgency of other people's emergencies as if they were my own? Why do I allow the institution's priorities to override my own? Why do I advocate for students, colleagues, and the institution, but not for myself?*

I began negotiating with others instead of complaining about them behind their backs. I began saying "no" and suffering colleagues' disapproval, instead of saying "yes" and suffering myself. When I accept work that is both unpalatable and unavoidable, I try to give it only the energy it deserves and no more, not even the energy of complaint or gossip. I'm always just beginning this work, and I still acquiesce at times, but I see a path beyond being stuck and stressed, and I head back toward it when I wander away. With plain common sense, Eckhart Tolle advises about difficulties, accept it, change it, or leave.[7] I'd like to keep my job, so I exercise the other two options as consciously as I can.

Despite the gas gauge warning, Helen's car kept on rolling into the woods and back out again a week later. A group of women faculty camped for a week, portaging in and out of the Boundary Waters Canoe Area, a wilderness area in northern Minnesota. I prepared myself for privation with a few items of clothing, as much waterproof outerwear as I owned, and, for indulgence, one book. One camper was celebrating her birthday, and I assumed a round of "Happy Birthday to You" and the first serving of reconstituted soup was all we'd offer her. Instead of this and in spite of the rain that had been drizzling for two days, Helen pulled out a skillet and a few baggies of ingredients, and baked a chocolate cake on a small propane camping stove. She decorated it with waterlogged candles, offering color instead of flame.

In both her professional and personal life, Helen knew how to finagle abundance from environments of scarcity. Watching her bake that cake, I marveled at the forethought and organization it took to carry a week's provisions on her back, even making room for a birthday celebration made even more meaningful by its superfluity.

I remembered that I had some of those skills, too, learned as a steakhouse waitress. In fact, looking at my professor career through a waitress's lens isn't entirely a bad idea. When the restaurant was busy, I had to bundle tasks (collect three forks, two drinks, a napkin, two straws, and a bill) in order to serve five or seven tables simultaneously. I had to focus, so I could remember orders and details from numerous customers. I had to prioritize

7. Tolle, *Practicing the Power of Now*.

when demands couldn't all be met immediately (scrape Jell-O off the carpet later, wipe dripping soda off the edge of a booth now). It even made me happy to find ways to make do in a chaotic environment. Of course, the stakes weren't very high. I knew I wouldn't waitress very long, because I was just making money for college. The strains and choices are heightened when a job or career will last years, and its demands seem incompatible with, say, sleeping, or mental health.

I don't know anyone who masters the art of balancing, or juggling. Even if one is able to perceive and prioritize the needs of students, colleagues, the institution, one's own physical and mental health, and family and home life, any one of these things will rise up to demand more, and not with good timing. The juggling metaphor, of course, pictures the juggler at the center of the frame. We often focus on the coping skills of the individual, when the deeper problems that cause the stress lie within the profession itself and its broader context. Individuals work around challenges as best they can, but the collective cost of everyone scrambling to "make do" is resulting in well-trained and skilled teachers leaving for other work, others staying in a permanent state of burnout, and widespread chronic stress and anxiety that wounds our hearts, our immune systems, and our lives outside of work.

Nonetheless, I'd like to earn a reputation like Helen's, being known as someone who says both "yes" and "no." This doesn't mean using the privilege of tenure and full professorship to be a faculty free rider; rather, it's setting boundaries in a workplace environment where the outer limits of the job are fuzzy, the institution's needs are endless, and the broader economic pressures are relentless and insane. Professor McDaniel concluded, "I like my work, it's just more than I can do well. I've had to give up on a lot of things, and I haven't done it for profit, I've done it for sanity."

6

Define the Relationship

My teachers take care of me.

—COLE, PRESCHOOLER

Teachers are there to help kids learn.

—MACEY, KINDERGARTENER

Feeling the energy of a passionate teacher is inspiring. We get to
inspire each other when we are together in person.

—SIMON, COLLEGE STUDENT

The term may not be widespread, but at my college, the "Define the
Relationship" talk, or the DTR, is a thing to behold. The DTR may
be anticipated with excitement (*Have you had the DTR yet? I think
we will soon!*) or it can be a sign of impending demise (*I think we're going
to have to have a DTR*). A DTR involves mutual discussion of the nature of

the relationship, and when it goes well, allows both people to proceed with agreed-upon parameters and depth of commitment.

I had a DTR of sorts with an undergraduate recently. I pondered this chapter with Tim, one of my advisees double majoring in Sociology/Anthropology and English. I said, "I think friendship is probably the best metaphor for the bond between teacher and student. It's not exactly like that, but it's a rough fit."

His expression shifted immediately from interest to worry, or perhaps pity. "Dr. Paris," he warned, "I really don't think you should put that in your book. You and I are not friends."

Friendship is about mutuality, equality, and shared experience, he said. Friends are there for each other. They do stuff together. He doesn't relate with his professors in these ways, nor does he want to. The friendship metaphor obscures power relations: by virtue of age, credentials, institutional position, and grading, teachers have more power, and they need to manage the flow of power differently than in a friendship between equals.

He concluded, "If what you're going for is a positive relationship with students, one that is caring and whatever, then yeah, that's a good teacher. The relationship is friendly, but don't turn that adverb into a noun."

I explained to him that while reading the history of one of the schools I'd attended, I came across a speech by the founder. He, an early twentieth-century philosopher-turned-college president, said that at its best, the bond between teacher and student is one of genuine friendship.

"Who were the teachers? Who were the students?" he questioned.

"Well, I hadn't thought about that. The teachers were Swedish immigrant male pastors and theologians, and their students were Swedish immigrant young men working to become pastors and theologians."

In that arrangement, friendship was likely both metaphor and reality, as students graduated to serve alongside their teachers in their immigrant communities. But in educational settings that include a greater age difference, and plurality of genders, religions, and life backgrounds, well, not so much.

"All right, Tim," I conceded. "Let's not be friends."

Though educational settings are diverse, and relationships between teachers and students vary accordingly, taking responsibility for defining the relationship constitutes a spiritual practice of love. It is loving to consider the perspectives and interests of others, especially when those others have less power within a given organizational setting. Apart from conversations such as the one I had with Tim, students generally don't overhear or participate in teacher-student DTRs, but they benefit from education that is grounded in a healthy and appropriate understanding of the teacher-student dynamic. In fearful times, we can find grounding by being clear about who we are in our role as teachers. What is the bond between teacher and student, at its best? Where are its boundaries, and how can we mark and maintain them?

I asked a similar question of a class of first-year college students in a seminar devoted to acclimating them to college. I said, "I earned a PhD by learning a lot of stuff and writing a dissertation about all that stuff. I teach classes where I share that stuff. But now that the Internet exists, why am I still here?" I pointed out the obvious: if what they want is to learn about anthropology, writing, qualitative research methods, gender relations, or anything else in my bag of tricks, they can download a lecture from iTunes University or YouTube and learn from the preeminent experts in the world. I posted this in-class writing exercise on the classroom screen.

What use is a teacher?

My fears were proven true, but in only a few responses.

- *In the year I took off college, I learned and grew more than I have here in school. I lived in the world doing practical things that impacted my life in a positive way. My mind was stretched with questions and struggles that really matter. But that won't get me anywhere in this life. I have to have a degree, so I'm here. To answer your question, I have no idea what the purpose of a professor is, but I appreciate that you would struggle with it, too.*

- *College is a social norm; without college, it's hard to get a good job. Personally, I'm here so I can continue on to med school one day. I believe we go to college to get a degree and eventually succeed, not to savor the wisdom and mentoring of a professor.*

In this view, teachers are bridge trolls, granting or denying passage to students who pass through our territory. *Answer me three riddles: an e-portfolio, a term paper, and a test, and you can pass!*

Teachers, or more pointedly, the grades that we assign, are what stand between students and their scholarships, their degrees, and to some extent, their futures. As service workers in a credentialing institution, our job seems to be to reward the paying customer with a passing grade (or a very high grade, for that matter, if that's what their scholarship or self-esteem requires). Whether with tax dollars or tuition, students and their families pay dearly, and there's lots of pressure from students, parents, and even sometimes our schools, for us to make their passage smooth.

To the contrary, nearly all the other students expressed very high expectations for teachers. Expectations surely vary with context, this one being a small residential liberal arts college where students are promised low teacher-student ratios, small classes, and a full-bodied cocurricular experience.

From various notecards:

- Teachers should *elaborate, plant knowledge, be devoted to me,* and *be someone to talk to.*

- A good teacher *makes it personable, holds me accountable,* and *inspires me.*

- *The most influential and memorable teachers form relationships with students and help them on their journey in life.*

Another student kindly pointed out the value of a teacher being a human being.

Teachers are invaluable because they are people. They are much better than books or an Internet search engine; they can help you, or at least move you in the right direction to get help.

My friends' children offered more ideas.

A sixth grader says teachers "get us ready for later life, they help us be successful."

A first grader says her teacher "helps me learn new stuff."

And a fourth grader, eyes opened to the game, says, "My teacher gets us ready for the state standardized assessments."

Interesting, too, what they didn't say. From preschoolers to college seniors, students didn't say they want teachers to entertain them. They didn't ask that teachers use clickers and embed video in their power points, or that we even try to match the technological aptitude of younger generations. They didn't ask for more precise assessments, measurable course objectives, or standardized tests. They didn't ask for professors to write more books or to produce cutting-edge knowledge. There's a place for all this, surely, but it's not center stage.

They're asking us to be human, to be present, and to care. To look at their faces and know their names. To select ideas, books, and assignments that are meaningful, and hold them accountable for staying the course. To inspire them with our knowledge, wisdom, and experience. To let them feel the energy and passion we have for the subject. To prepare them for what's next, though neither they nor we know what that might be.

Despite my good intentions, I turned bridge troll with Andriano, a senior undergraduate. I was supervising his internship, part of a Washington, DC semester program for college students pursuing public service. He was required to attend the internship, which he did enthusiastically, and complete the academic portion of the internship (attending class and writing a final paper), which he ignored altogether.

When he realized his grade was looking dismal, Andriano asked to meet with me. I agreed, and when we met, he asked if we could go for a walk because it was a nice day. I didn't own a car, but he did, and he drove us to an isolated part of Rock Creek Park. He offered deep conversation about his world view, family, and aspirations—material for a good integrative paper, had he opted to write one. He showed intense interest in my feedback, despite having skipped my lectures and never having conversed with me before. On an old stone bride that passed over a gurgling creek, he stopped and looked me full in the eyes.

"Let me take you to lunch, Jenell, on me."

Yikes!, I realized, *He's wooing me! And it's not love he's after; rather, he wants his grade raised.*

I said I needed to get back to campus. After I processed the encounter for a few days, including talking it over with a colleague who agreed it sounded like grade-related flirtation, I became enraged. I met with Andriano again, in my office with the door open, and plainly recounted his academic failures. I assigned him such a low grade for his internship that the program director asked me to change it. He had, after all, put in long hours at the internship with rave reviews from his supervisor. He also had paid good money to come to our program, and we needed future students to come from his college. I refused. I insisted that I was being objective and fair, when in fact I was taking it personally, feeling humiliated and uncertain, wondering whether I sent signals that I would bend to flattery.

I might have discussed the walk in Rock Creek Park, offered my view, listened to his, and advised him about how to better handle gender relations in the workplace. I could have brought in the program director to listen to us both. I could have coordinated with the program director, other faculty, or his internship director, to jointly advise and teach Andriano. His grade may or may not have changed, but I could have offered more clear options for him to change course, and held him accountable.

Instead, I was the troll under the bridge. *You failed to answer my third riddle, so you will never cross over.*

My insistence on giving him the lowest grade possible was about my revenge, not Andriano's welfare. I disguised vindictiveness with a veneer of fairness and professionalism, a disguise that I entirely believed. The program director changed Andriano's grade from disastrous to mediocre, the one and only time a superior has overridden my grading.

Setting and maintaining healthy boundaries with students is, or should be, a perennial topic of conversation among teachers. How much should we self-disclose about our personal lives, our beliefs, our doubts? How and under what circumstances, if ever, should we touch students? Should we talk with students with office door open or shut? How far into our families and personal lives should they come? When romantic or sexual potential presents itself, under what circumstances (if any) and with what cautions should it be pursued? Just how literally should they "feel our energy"?

This is perhaps the simplest, yet the most profound, truth of all. The fundamental reason for teaching is to help someone learn something . . . when you reflect on your skill as a teacher, there is only one fundamental question you need to ask: Are my actions helping students learn?

—STEPHEN BROOKFIELD[1]

Guidelines for teacher-student relationships may be explicit, stated by schools or by law, especially for younger ages. In higher education settings, the legal bounds of harassment, consent, and violence govern relations between adults, including adults who happen to be professors or students. Universities have different standards for amorous relationships: they are often generally discouraged, forbidden when a student and faculty are in a context where a grading or evaluative relationship is underway,

1. Brookfield, *Skillful Teacher*, 210.

or forbidden altogether. General though it is, I appreciate my professional association's guidance, offered in the American Anthropological Association's code of ethics. "In relations with students, anthropologists should be candid, fair, nonexploitative, and committed to the student's welfare and progress."[2]

It can sometimes be healthy for boundaries to flex and shift as a relationship grows over time. Though he used to be more formal, my student Darrell comes in my office, kicks off his shoes, and lays across two chairs, making himself as comfortable as possible as he launches into a new dimension of his ever-changing life philosophy. Kathy comes into my home to photograph my children, her work doing double duty as photography class assignment and gift to me. In other contexts, boundaries are fixed. My friend's daughter came home on the first day of kindergarten complaining, "The teacher says she doesn't give hugs or kisses!"

When they teach us from their expertise, offer new data and perspectives, or even give support in times of personal crisis, the student becomes the teacher. And when we really listen to students, pursue conversations in which something real is at stake for us, or lean on them as guides to a rapidly changing society, the teacher becomes the student. But even then, as Tim reminded me, the teacher remains on the heavier side of the power dynamic.

I worried when my colleague Tom complained to me about limitations in his relationship with a nineteen-year-old student. "Why can't we just have a human encounter, without the trappings of professional roles? She really gets me. When I'm with her, it's like we're just two perfectly matched souls."

I argued, "But you're twice her age, and you're married, and you're her supervisor. She needs employment and mentoring, not a soul mate."

We debated, and he didn't talk to me about the student again, but later he was dismissed from the college after she complained. From what I could gather, she went along with the deepening friendship, but then said it felt creepy and wrong when he offered to rent her an apartment where they could be together. After processing the situation with her parents and with a counselor, she thought that, despite her willingness to cross boundaries, he should have protected them.

The teacher-student relationship is, first and foremost, about the student. Tom's pursuit of a soul mate was for his benefit, not the student's. As

2. "Statement of Ethics."

an undergraduate, I connected with Dr. Sanna, who soon became John, as we found shared areas of interest, senses of humor, and professional aspirations (I wanted to be a good professor someday, and he said he did, too). I spent time hanging out at his house, observed him playing with his children as well as disciplining them, and being kind to his wife as well as negotiating with her or even apologizing. He listened to the intricacies of my family and romantic relationships, and sometimes shared comparable stories from his own life.

In retrospect, I can see that he revealed himself to me only to the extent that it was helpful to me, and that he was careful about privacy and intimacy. For example, "hanging out at his house" seemed spontaneous to me at the time, but now I can see it wasn't coincidence that we were never alone there: he only invited me over when his wife and kids were around. It was a real, human connection, but it didn't need to burst the bonds of social roles in order to pursue a more true connection; in fact, the relationship thrived because it respected the boundaries of those roles. I wouldn't call John my soul mate; rather, he was something even better matched with my student self: my teacher.

Tom's desire to pursue a "human encounter" with a student, free of role constraints, was not naïve; rather, it was self-delusion. Just as I didn't see myself slip into revenge as I graded Andriano's work, Tom's mentoring of a student slipped into an attempt to use her to meet a desire for intimacy that wasn't being met by his peers.

My program director spoke the truth that could have corrected my self-delusion, but I was unwilling to hear it. I stood on my moral high ground for several years until I was willing to face the fact that I had put my own needs ahead of a student's. I came to hold my failure with compassion: I was a brand-new professor, eager to defend my authority. It was the first time I'd been in a situation like that. I get angry when men cross me. And I can have compassion toward Andriano, too. He was trying to get a good grade without doing the work. That's unwise, but it's not a capital offense. And if he's inclined to treat female superiors inappropriately, better to try it in college with a professor who might be instructive, than in a workplace where the consequences could be much more severe.

When I was in junior high, my sister and I used to talk my parents into driving past Mr. Sutton's house. He was a biology teacher and we both took his class, though in different years. We'd imagine how he might live in his house, what he might eat for supper, or whether or not he had a pet. One time he was outside raking his yard and we laid down on the back seat as our parents drove past, laughing our heads off.

We weren't laughing at Mr. Sutton—he was one of our favorite teachers. It was just so weird, seeing that he lived in a house, with a family, and that he did yard work. It was like he was a person or something.

Weird, too, that my student said he likes the fact that his teachers are human. Part of the reason for attending class with a real teacher instead of downloading virtual lectures, he wrote, is that it matters that the teacher is a person. Modern professionalism, maybe especially in the helping professions, can reduce or even eliminate humanity by turning people into clients, numbers, units, or cases. Psychologist Carl Rogers wrote,

> In the clinical areas we develop elaborate diagnostic formulations, seeing the person as an object. In teaching and in administration we develop all kinds of evaluative procedures, so that again the person is perceived as an object. In these ways, I believe, we can keep ourselves from experiencing the caring which would exist if we recognized the relationship as one between two persons. It is a real achievement when we can learn even in certain relationships or at certain times in those relationships, that it is safe to care, that it is safe to relate to the other as a person for whom we have positive feelings.[3]

Perhaps the relationship between teacher and student needs no metaphor: it simply is what it is. The teacher should teach. When we slip into friendship, romantic intimacy, personal revenge, or self-protection, we are doing something other than teaching. A teacher should take no more from students than delight and satisfaction in having given her best. For their part, students should study—learn, watch, explore, advance in understanding and wisdom. When they do something other than that—care for their professor's feelings, step up to become a supposed equal in friendship or intimacy, they are doing something other than studying. Political scientist Hugh Heclo explains that the actions of teachers should be in harmony with the purpose of the institution. "Practice will inevitably fall short. Other agendas will intervene. But in the relationship between teacher and student, the one with the assumed authority of a teacher and the other with the need and opportunity of a student to learn, this is the basic institutional

3. Rogers, "Characteristics," 13.

aspiration by which we know we are falling short and being distracted by other agendas."[4]

The spiritual practice is defining the relationship, a practice that is ongoing as we age, as personal and professional circumstances change, and as we meet new students. While most teachers don't slip up as egregiously as Tom did, we all fall short, at times allowing other agendas to shape how we treat students, agendas such as wanting to be seen as authoritative or smart, wanting to be liked, or simply wanting to get home by a certain time. Correcting course, however slightly or dramatically, is an ongoing part of the wise teacher's journey.

The questions are, *Who am I as a teacher? Who are students, for me? Who am I, to them?* By defining the relationship—in our own minds, in conversation with colleagues, and in compliance with law—we don't diminish the spark of human connection or make our relations coldly bureaucratic. We can strive to be teachers who are candid, fair, nonexploitative, and committed to the student's welfare and progress. Whether the relationship is counselor to client, as Carl Rogers describes, or teacher to student, honoring the personhood of both, with all associated responsibilities and boundaries, can open up a space for a real, caring bond between two human beings.

In the end, I agree with Tim. Aiming for "a positive relationship with students, one that is caring and whatever, then yeah, that's a good teacher."

---

4. Heclo, *On Thinking Institutionally,* 132.

7

Make It by Hand

Why choose to be a teacher? Because teaching is not only a thing of skill but an art; not only a thing into which one puts knowledge but also into which one puts creativity and imagination.

—Dorothy Baruch, *Why Teach?*

A s the last chapter described, some teachers are tempted to become best friends, soul mates, or lovers with students: stories along those lines are not hard to come by in the news and in our schools. If you're not so tempted, it may be easy to judge from a distance. *I would never! How could they?* Breaches of law and ethics are not the only distortions of role to which teachers fall prey, however. Most teachers—perhaps all—are pushed and pulled to distortion as education at all levels increasingly relies on business logic: students are customers, teachers are service providers, and education itself is commodity. Teachers provide services according to economies of scale and standardization of service provision across the industry, with massive administrative, legislative, and regulatory structures guiding this education "economy." As a curriculum manager at a for-profit university explained to me, "We just can't afford to let professors design their own classes. We need to control quality so students know what they're buying. So we have project managers and techies design the classes, and hire professors to deliver them."

Modern education is only in part a pursuit of truth, goodness, and justice. It also serves the nation, which needs citizens to be productive (as defined by the economic needs at any given moment), competitive, and to some extent, compliant. Strange blends of the free spirit of learning mixed with the nation's task of producing citizens change over time. In the twentieth century, regulation, including accreditation, helped cohere a vast hodgepodge of schools and make quality more recognizable for incoming students and for employers. It also helped advance the rising demand for universal literacy and high school completion. At present, however, a decades-long collaboration between business and political leaders is dampening what ought to be a generative tension between the status quo's need to maintain itself and the sometimes disruptive impulses of truth, freedom, and creativity.

Teachers (and doctors, plumbers, electricians, and all other skilled workers) are rightfully artisans, not service providers. A health care service provider may be trained with a script, even a complex script that includes an index to many different complaints or situations, but this is not the same as healing. An educational service provider may deliver content that was vetted, focus-grouped, and packaged by techies and managers, but this is not teaching. That so many doctors and teachers are able to heal and to teach even in these ridiculous situations is testament to their mastery of their craft. I called a nurse line recently, and thankfully got a nurse wise enough to know when to break script.

"My son has a rash," I said, "I'm not sure what to do."

I heard the click of keyboarding as she typed "rash" into her computer. She read a list of scripted questions related to color, location, itchiness, and so on.

"Do I need to take him in to a doctor?" I wanted to know. "I have two other kids, and I'd have to wake them all up and drag them along, and I don't want to unless it's really necessary."

The script offered careful words, surely vetted by a lawyer, seemingly crafted more to articulate legal liabilities than to help the patient. The nurse read the script, then said, "Look, my kid had that rash too. Just keep an eye on it and go in if it gets worse."

An artisan knows how to read not just a script, but to read a situation, read a person, and see what is called for. Just because the numbers on the dial are accurate, or the rubric adds up, or the assessment grid met its "pass" standard, doesn't mean all is well. An artisan learns the feel of quality, the taste of completion, and the smell of trouble by relying on her senses, intuition, and experience, as well as on her education and training. Artisans certainly make mistakes, a possibility always visible when we see the person who is making the calls. Computers, big data, and spreadsheets make mistakes too, but their façade of objectivity lowers our guard against that inevitability.

In the interest of strengthening education, teachers spend increasing amounts of time and energy on things other than teaching, like reporting, assessing, and test-prepping. In the interest of passing tests and earning credentials, students invest increasing amounts of time and energy in tasks that merely simulate learning, such as doing that, and only that, which will secure them a certain number in a certain box on a certain rubric. In the interest of shaping children into functional, competent adult human beings, we diminish vital human elements of education such as subjectivity, creativity, open-endedness, and exploration.

As a college professor in a field that doesn't offer program accreditation or even standardized tests for undergraduate or graduate competence, I am positioned further from the customer service model than most other teachers. I choose my own books, design my own class sessions, and grade according to standards I've developed. Yet I see the effects in students arriving from K–12 education: their valuing of testable material over all else, clamoring for rubrics, and reluctance to stray from teacher-guided material into the big world of ideas. When my twins were in second grade, one climbed about thirty feet up a climbing wall. The other shouted up at him, "If there was a rubric for this, you'd get a ten!"

I'm even further away from these pressures in community education, where I teach card making once or twice a year. It couldn't be simpler: students spend an hour and a half a day, for five days, making cards. I bring ideas, principles of design, paper, stickers, and glue sticks. They bring fantastic energy, high expectations, and lots of goodwill. They're always on time, and there are no discipline issues. I have to make them leave when class is over; they'd stay for hours. The incentive structure is different than in school, and it shows. They don't need grades or credits, and they don't turn their work in to me for evaluation. They've voluntarily paid money to learn something of interest to them, something that has no instrumental value toward their careers or financial well-being.

One student volunteers in hospice, and was developing a line of cards that volunteers can make by hand for families facing the loss of a loved one. He wrote what I first took as a hyperbolic thank-you: "Please know that your course has made a giant impact on your students as each one of us will further the art of card making. Giving something homemade is simply a lost art."

Giant impact? Art? I'm just crafty, expert in refrigerator magnets, macramé lawn chairs, and spray-painted pine cones. But my students respond to card making with genuine enthusiasm, often grateful simply to have received time, materials, and permission to make something by hand. And whether or not the market would judge their work as worthy, they are artists: doing meaningful work with their own hands, turning basic materials into something unique, and making an object that reflects the maker's whole-hearted investment in it.

Writing nearly seventy years ago, educator Dorothy Baruch summed up why many teachers choose to teach still today. We want to be both skilled workers, offering knowledge and skill, and also artists who share creativity and imagination.

Why, then, does the Department of Education define a "highly effective teacher" as "a teacher whose students achieve high rates (e.g., one and one-half grade levels in an academic year) of student growth (as defined in this notice)." Student growth is "the change in student achievement (as defined in this notice) for an individual student between two or more points in time." Student achievement may be measured in various ways, but for testable subjects, must include "a student's score on the State's assessments under the ESEA [Elementary and Secondary Education Act]."[1] In short, while they may also do other things as well, the defining characteristic of a highly effective teacher is that her students pass state assessments.

Who would choose to teach for that reason? What good teacher would exchange excellence for effectiveness, the joy of learning for the passing of tests?

When the subject is standardized testing, common standards, and compliance with these kinds of federal regulations, I hear good teachers talk about their hearts: their hearts are breaking, they are losing heart, they

---

1. "Race to the Top."

are despairing and tiring. They feel distrusted and misunderstood, even vilified. They try to offer their best, but it isn't wanted or valued. A friend retired early from public teaching after a thirty-year career, saying today's pressures and constraints are too crazy-making, and the opportunities for her to make a difference are too few. Another worries about making it sixteen more years to retirement, and is sad that new teachers only know this status quo.

I see teachers and schools scrambling to boost scores. I see math and English drilled into kids, with seemingly everything else either treated as nonessential luxuries or judged by ill-fitting measures. I receive notices of test performance that report my children's abilities with indecipherable graphs and acronyms. I see the shaming effect of school comparisons posted in area newspapers.

A special ed teacher posted online his "Dear John" letter, a sincere expression of a teacher's heartbreak.[2]

> Dear Special Ed,
>
> I'm writing to break up with you, to tell you that I don't love you anymore.
>
> To be fair, I loved you when we first met. I remember how I used to work with kids who were incredibly withdrawn, who had no idea what their potential was, and how much a gift to me it was to see a child begin to believe in herself. I remember kids getting excited about learning, kids who actually began to laugh louder and more often from excitement and self-pride. I remember the spark in their eyes when they knew how to solve a problem that before had been just a mystery. I remember fondly that kid who said, "You are like a dad to me" and that girl who said, "You have always been there for me." I wept the day a young differently abled woman told me her dream is to work with immigrants to help them.
>
> But Special Ed, I failed to see something in you from the beginning, something that I glossed over because I was so focused on helping kids to build a better future when I first began. You really don't care about the kids like I thought you did.
>
> [When w]e first met, I thought that your need to have me spend so much time writing legal paperwork was just a foible of yours. I thought, "Okay, Special Ed, you'll come around." Then I thought, "well, now that I can write Johnny's legal paperwork online, I'll be able to spend more time with Johnny." I even tried for years to see

2. Personal correspondence.

if I could get you to change, but Special Ed, I was wrong. You are more needy now than ever before and your insatiable demands for me to prove that I've done my job have gotten so out of hand that I have little time left to actually teach Johnny or think about how best to teach him. You want to measure everything, regardless of how valuable it is for a child. You want to report, report, report every measurement, regardless of what Johnny is doing while I'm working on the report. You take Johnny out of class so many times during the year and stun him with a statewide test that it makes me think of you as an abuser of children.

"Johnny? Johnny who?" you might be asking.

Let me introduce you to Johnny. He's not an IEP. He's not a Notice of Team Meeting. He's not an educational plan. Johnny is an exceptional child who has very particular needs, needs that will not actually be met or addressed if Johnny's teachers must spend time trying to appease you, Special Ed. Johnny is a human being, who is often highly vulnerable and whose needs can be so significant, that failure to meet them could be described as a matter of life or death.

So I'm leaving you as soon as I can. I won't leave Johnny. I'll do my best to find him in other class settings where I can actually help him, but you? Forget about it. You've gotten in between me and the kids I'm so passionate about teaching and I won't stand for it any longer than the two more years it'll take to get a new license.

Sincerely,
Special Jim

None of this seems good for children, families, or society. It certainly doesn't seem highly effective. Maybe Star Trek got it right. When the Borg encountered opponents, they'd send this message: "We are the Borg. Lower your shields and surrender your ships. We will add your biological and technological distinctiveness to our own. Your culture will adapt to service us. Resistance is futile."[3]

And yet.

And yet my children love their teachers. They bring their teachers trinkets and drawings and accidentally call them "Mom." And their teachers love them. They notice their students' individuality: new shoes, a new band-aid covering a new owie, or a step forward in reading. They turn lessons into songs, games, and puppet shows. One tells the students about

3. Movie Fanatic.

the antics of her cats; another, her new grandbaby. This isn't time off task, away from objectives and outcomes and goals. It is the art of teaching, the idiosyncratic, skilled, and human work that makes strong bonds of trust and joy that are absolutely necessary for real learning. Drilling "objective" material may turn kids into federally approved test-takers, but it takes love to help them become whole, happy, and secure human beings.

Psychologist Carl Rogers emphasized the importance of a teacher's "realness." The teacher

> becomes a real person in the relationship with his students . . . . He is a *person*, not a faceless embodiment of a curricular requirement, or a sterile pipe through which knowledge is passed from one generation to the next . . . . As I think back over a number of teachers who have facilitated my own learning, it seems to me each one has this quality of being a real person. I wonder if your memory is the same. If so, perhaps it is less important that a teacher cover the allotted amount of the curriculum, or use the most approved audio-visual devices, than that he be congruent, real, in his relation to his students.[4]

Despite the incursion of the Borg, teachers resist. Sometimes administrators and entire schools do, too. For the most part it is not an organized resistance, but rather, insistence and persistence in being not only highly effective, but being good. As defined by Baruch, a good teacher relishes art, creativity, and inspiration. As defined by Rogers, a good teacher is a real person, congruent in relation to students. And as defined by any student who ever had one, a good teacher is excited about what he does, does it well, and cares about students.

Though the pressures to standardize inputs and homogenize outputs have never been stronger, masterful teaching and deep learning can't be churned out like processed food on a factory conveyor belt. It can't be forced (or in my opinion, adequately measured) with rubrics, outcomes, goals, measures, evaluations, quantifications, or standardizations. Like students themselves, learning can be encouraged and shaped, but it can't be controlled.

There is a quality to education that is sensory. A master teacher feels her way through the process, constantly rebalancing challenge and support, content and process, constraint and freedom. Students know when they are

4. Rogers, "Significant Learning," 106–7.

being led by a good teacher because they feel it: they feel energized, cared for, woken up.

Good teachers are artisans in a world of mass-produced, over-processed education. The adjective "artisanal" is sometimes used in describing hand processing in what is usually viewed as an industrial process. In a documentary about Belgian beer brewing, a master artisan guides an apprentice in establishing his own brewery. Small brewery owners are enthusiastically generous when a newcomer wants to learn the craft. The artisan had the phenotype and facial hair of Santa Claus, with wide eyes and a quick smile. He explained the steps of beer brewing, stopping at one point to inspect a dial.

"This dial is at the right number, but you still have to taste it."

He and the apprentice taste, and the master holds his reaction until the apprentice offers one, eyebrows scrunched in disappointment.

"See, the taste tells you it isn't quite right, so it needs a small adjustment."

"It's all about science," Santa Claus concluded, and then flashed a big smile, "except really, it's an art!"

Artisanry doesn't require total freedom and autonomy. In fact, it assumes mass production as a point of contrast: you recognize the value of artisanal cheese, in part, because you've tasted Velveeta. Artisans use handwork when it makes good sense, and they also rely on mainstream market production and supply of materials and tools, not to mention the housing, roads, and public utilities that their life and work depend on. Artisans keep their craft alive and viable in the midst of a market economy.

Likewise, there is no teaching from scratch. Educators who see education as a means of social mobility, global poverty reduction, and universal literacy need governments and large funding structures to even begin to work toward these goals. And, realistically, the vast majority of teachers will spend their careers within mainstream systems. Even when teachers create a new charter school, or homeschool, we still rely on the broader society for electricity, building supplies, and the like, as well as the shared words, symbols, rituals, and behaviors that constitute our culture. Artisans practice their skills in contexts that both enable and constrain: in comparison to industrial production, they work more slowly, doing more by hand, and putting more of themselves into their work. They both rely upon and push against mainstream systems.

As part of his master's degree at the Royal College of Art in London, Thomas Thwaites set out to make a toaster from scratch. First, he deconstructed a toaster and listed its parts, all four hundred of them. Then he traveled to mines to extract and produce steel, mica, copper, and nickel. He made plastic, too, at home in a cooking pot. Over nine months he traveled nineteen hundred miles and spent $1,800 to make a toaster that looks like something a cave man made, and then melted. It warms bread, but cannot toast it.

His conclusion is one that he surely could have reached in the first place with a simple thought experiment, though that wouldn't have been nearly as fun. "[A]lthough I set out to make my toaster completely from scratch, I realised along the way that there can be no such thing as 'from scratch.'"[5] Even to extract minerals from a mine, Thwaites had to get dressed, drive his car, and email and call the mine, all of which involve complex materials and technologies. In producing metals and plastics, he used cooking pots and tools that were developed by others.

Acknowledgement of necessary dependence upon the very systems we critique can yield deeper understanding of the broader world. In the book's introduction, David Crowley writes, "Making a toaster from scratch is surely an impossible task, but not a pointless one. Thwaites's project reveals much about the organisation of the modern world, not least the extent to which Britain's industrial capacity has been dismantled. The country's mines, foundries, and factories have become, it seems, another form of phantasmagoria."[6]

Some teachers retire early or leave for other lines of work. Some succumb, working in bitterness and despair. Others remain in the system, but manage to keep their artisanry alive. They work by hand when they're able, and when it makes sense. What do they make? Depending on the constraints and freedoms of a particular school, and depending on the skills and interests of the teacher, they may hand-make assignments, games, puppet shows, equations and proofs, and baking soda volcanoes. They make connections with students and parents, colleagues, and administrators. They make book choices, syllabi, student assessments, and final grade evaluations. They make seating arrangements and order of activities and classroom decorations and holiday observances and opportunities for

5. Thwaites, *Toaster Project*, 15.
6. Ibid., 12.

student discussion. They are "highly effective" teachers because they have to be. They are good teachers because they want to be.

Teaching from scratch may be impossible, but teaching as an artisan, working by hand whenever possible within an industry dominated by mass production and standardization and misplaced notions of quality, is far from pointless. We are able to teach even more effectively about the organization of the modern world when students see us struggling with some of its most poignant tensions. It seems ever harder, with constraints that bear down on the micro level of our teaching days, but artisan teachers will always keep practicing their craft, honing their skill in tactile and sensory ways, learning to blend innovation and tradition, idiosyncrasy and conformity, personal expression and compliance with regulation.

If teachers are artisans, what are students? They aren't apprentices in any literal sense; there are simply too many of them in a year, a semester, or even in a single class. And most of them are not working toward mastery in our domain. For me, it's far less than one each year who wishes to earn a doctorate in my discipline. But we don't teach our subjects: we teach students. We guide them toward mastery of living a well-considered life. This is sometimes transcendent, looking in the world for reflections of platonic ideals of goodness, justice, and beauty. Perhaps more often it is immanent, embedded in our subjects. In anthropology, the juiciest parts are about what it means to be human, how people are different and the same, how culture and context shapes our lives, and the dynamics of in/equality and in/justice around the world. As we immerse ourselves in the topic at hand, students learn to do more than fiddle a dial or follow a script. They begin to work a process, to embody a tradition and relish its nuances. They become "someone learning," which is what "apprentice" means.[7]

At its best, schooling can be about how to make a life, which is quite different from how to make a living.

—Neil Postman[8]

---

7. Online Etymology Dictionary, "Apprentice."

8. Postman, *End of Education*, x.

Students can be our apprentices, but only when they want to be. When they insist on being customers, and many of them will, let them purchase something handcrafted, of lasting value, something that they had a hand in making. They will pay dearly with tuition dollars, time, and attention, and it will be worth it.

One of our paramount tasks in the world today is to strive to live well within massive depersonalized systems that are broken, corrupt, or inefficient—often ravenously so. It' is good that our students see us struggle to teach them well. The tensions and breaks in educational systems can serve as a lens for students to see difficult truths about their world. After all, most of them will end up working in mainstream organizations and industries, in a society that threatens to commodify the things they hold most dear, even their bodies, faces, and selves. The business model may dominate their education, but at the same time, students can see and experience how human economies can still thrive within them when we cultivate careful, local, highly skilled, and humane processes of making and using things like material objects, values, relationships, and ideas.

The practice is to make it by hand. When possible and sensible, invest your whole self in certain parts of your teaching. Invite students to do the same, investing their whole selves in the parts of their education that are worthy of it. Whether it's a new assignment, lecture, approach to discipline, school-wide reform, or something else, our handmade efforts will often be slow, inefficient, difficult to replicate, and imperfect. We'll need to repeat them, get a feel for them, in order to make them really good. And as we do, we'll be proud that we've done it ourselves.

In card-making classes, I give permission to my students: it's OK to do it your own way. Find the colors and textures that you like, and go for it. Student self-critique often refer to mass-produced commercial cards:

It doesn't look professional, but I like it.

I know it isn't like the ones in the store.

Sadly, one of the highest compliments we crafters offer each other is, *You could sell this!* Even in the most free and autonomous spaces, we look to the market for estimations of value.

The market doesn't value the master teacher: her approach is too idiosyncratic, her labor too expensive, her output too unpredictable. If, in addition to getting your students to pass standardized tests, you also love them, know their names, laugh at their jokes, and look forward to seeing them after breaks, well, don't expect the system to value that. Some schools, administrators, and boards will, but many won't. Because it isn't quantified as a desirable and measurable outcome, artisanry is seen as optional, subjective, and of uncertain value.

The market seeks standardization of product that can be made, sold, delivered, and consumed *en masse*. Artisans produce in small batches, with skill gained from experience over time. The market measures quality, whereas the artisan feels it. An artisanal product is local and fresh, in some way a creative expression of its maker. June Taylor, artisan of fruit preserves, says, "a food artisan is someone who is completely and wholly integrated into the creation of their product."[9]

When you make it by hand, put your whole heart into it, and do it as only you can, it will surely be noticed and valued by the most important measure: the delight of your students.

9. Taylor, "What is artisanal food?"

8

Nurture Integrity

Power is of two kinds. One is obtained by the fear of punishment and the other by acts of love. Power based on love is a thousand times more effective and permanent than the one derived from fear of punishment.

—GANDHI

"Research shows that the most powerful way to discourage students from cheating is for a professor to look them in the eye and say that academic integrity matters to him or her. So look at me. Here I am, looking at you, saying that your academic integrity matters to me."

After this opener, I detail the college's academic integrity policy, its definitions and consequences, and offer to assist students as they navigate the details of appropriate collaboration and citation. I make this pitch in the first week of nearly every class I teach. I first heard it as an undergraduate in Dr. Kim's psychology class. It hit home: by cheating, I'd not only violate an abstract code of ethics, I'd also be offending a professor.

I've never investigated the veracity of Dr. Kim's claim, but I did investigate cheating in general, and it seems to be very common. James Lang reviewed available research and reached an unsurprising conclusion: it's clear as day that many students cheat. Experts debate over trends and specifics, but Lang summarizes, "I suspect we can all agree on one point: the rates of cheating are much higher than we want them to be."[1]

My friend wrote a letter to her children's high school, quoting her kids as saying, "Cheating is everywhere, Mom, from copying homework, to quizzes, to tests."

"Kids write answers on their arms, legs, clothing, fingers, bottoms of feet and shoes, and on the palms of their hands."

"Many teachers don't seem to notice even though it is right under their noses."

Experts recommend much more than teachers making earnest statements to students, though that is one contribution to strengthening educational cultures of integrity. Everyone involved in a student's education—parents, peers, teachers, support staff, and administrators—can work toward embedding honesty, respect, trust, and responsibility into school cultures.

This sounds difficult and it is, all the more when teachers and administrators also cheat. Sometimes the lines are unclear—does classroom power point material borrowed from a website or textbook publisher need to be cited? But other times, far too often, the lines are clear enough and are crossed anyway. Teachers and students cheat together on standardized tests. A faculty member publishes sentences or paragraphs from someone else's work without attribution. A university president delivers speeches that are cut and pasted from the Internet.

Integrity isn't about not cheating; rather, it means to be of sound and whole condition.[2] It's not merely catching cheating, though some teachers are loathe to do even that. It's not merely moralistic: consider the damage done to the global economy by the shortcuts and knowing deviance practiced on Wall Street and elsewhere. Nurturing integrity involves watching and understanding the environments and the personal dispositions that tend to result in cheating, and then altering the classroom environment and incentivizing individuals in ways that encourage everyone to do their own work.

The practice is to nurture integrity as part of a pedagogy of love. Love is not just rainbows and smiles. It is hearty enough to transform mistakes, even willful ones, into opportunities for learning and personal growth. When teachers ignore cheating, or address it only with punishment, we

1. Lang, *Cheating Lessons*, 15. See also Davis et al., *Cheating in School*.
2. Online Etymology Dictionary, "Integrity."

miss the chance to let love do its work. Love—for students, for integrity, and for the academic material at hand—helps us handle cheating by refusing its distractions. When students cheat, we may focus more on the student's misdoing than on her humanity, which is a distraction. Pursuing another distraction, we may focus more on preventing or terminating the cheating than on furthering the student's education. Love keeps us focused on the well-being of the student, and on our central task, which is to teach.

When teachers face themselves, they face a hard struggle; but they may also look forward to great rewards. The greatest of these rewards is growth in compassion.

—ARTHUR JERSILD[3]

Cheating calls for teachers to use their power. As Gandhi said, power is of two kinds. The power of punishment may stop cheating in a particular instance, but if it is the dominant approach, it merely trains students to do as they please, as long as they don't get caught. The power of love is both caring and clever, proactive and responsive. It is committed to restoring integrity, not merely stopping cheating. It is committed to teaching, not merely punishing. It is committed to the student's well-being. It is a thousand times more effective and permanent.

Perhaps he wasn't looking me in the eye when I delivered my pitch. Ian always sat in the back of Race, Ethnicity, and Peacemaking, dutifully doing whatever it was that he did during class. I never heard him speak. As business majors sometimes do, he dressed for the job he wanted, not the job he had. Normally he dressed for his future corporate job: shined shoes, pressed slacks, and a light-colored dress shirt, with the exception of casual Friday Dockers and a polo shirt. I could smell him coming or going; it was as if he lived under a cloud of cologne, and it was always misty. He was tall, strong, and blond, an archetypal Minnesotan of Scandinavian descent who, in another time and place, might have captained a Viking ship.

He turned in a paper that smelled a little like cologne and a lot like plagiarism. A sentence along the lines of, "Therefore, continued efforts at public enlightenment and extension of constitutional rights and equal

---

3. Jersild, *When Teachers Face Themselves*, 125.

opportunities to all Americans, regardless of race, religion, or national origin, appear to be the most promising means of attaining an unprejudiced society"[4] followed one like "There were tons of white kids in my high school." The paper jerked back and forth between doctoral-level jargon and plain English. Maybe Ian would have pirated that Viking ship, not captained it.

College policy required me to discuss the matter with the student, assign a consequence of my choosing, and file a report with the dean's office so, should a student cheat repeatedly, it would be documented and addressed. I asked colleagues and was surprised by the range of responses to cheating and plagiarism. A few gave failing grades on an assignment or an entire course with no discussion or opportunity for restoration. Others confronted cheating and gave opportunities for re-doing work for a reduced grade. I had once worked as a teaching assistant for one of the vigilant sorts and had to follow students to the restroom during exams to see if they really did have to go, or if they were checking notes they might have planted in the restroom trash or tucked behind a mirror. I also had to keep especially close watch on students with long-sleeved shirts (notes on forearms), baseball caps (notes on brims), or backpacks, which included just about everyone. I was surprised by the lengths to which some teachers went to catch cheating, but I was even more perplexed by those who did nothing. *It takes so much time to deal with it. I just try to not to notice it. Those confrontations with students are really uncomfortable. If they're going to cheat, they're going to cheat. Let them reap the consequences in the workplace.*

I took what I saw a middle road between, on the one hand, listening to students pee in the restroom, and on the other hand, doing nothing. I tracked down the original source (this took about five seconds because he copied from the class textbook I had assigned), highlighted plagiarized sections of the paper, and filled out the dean's paperwork. I met with Ian's academic advisor, who responded by leaning forward to cover his face with his hands.

"Aaaargh," he exhaled frustration, "sometimes they think 'ethics' is just one more class to cheat their way through." He promised to work closely with Ian, mentoring him toward ethical practice in his student years that could, hopefully, benefit his professional life. He agreed to be in the room when I met with Ian.

---

4. Parrillo, *Understanding Race*, 93.

When he saw us waiting for him, Ian blushed beet red. I showed him the paper and said, "This is a problem. This paper is plagiarized." "I wrote that," he insisted. I opened the textbook to the passages he had copied and he changed his story. "I didn't know I needed to cite it. I thought if it was less than a paragraph, it didn't have to be cited." He argued with me, but submitted to his academic advisor who used corporate language like "core values" and "organizational boundaries" to explain the gravity of Ian's error. I said he earned a zero on this assignment, and that while he could remain in the class, he should consider whether or not he wanted to.

Twenty minutes later, Ian reappeared in my doorway, taking up most of it. Red-faced with anger now instead of embarrassment, he raised his voice. "I can't believe you humiliated me in front of my advisor! I need letters of reference from him! You're trying to wreck my whole future!"

I insisted that academic advisors in general, and this one in particular, work for the good of students, and that Ian should stay in a mentoring relationship with him. His rant continued until I interrupted, "This is not OK. You can't speak to me like this. You need to leave." I told his advisor that Ian had been aggressive toward me, and I sent Ian a note saying he wasn't welcome back in my class.

This bad ending may have been inevitable, but maybe it wasn't. It's easy to blame Ian, easy to see junctures at which he could have made better decisions. Yet regardless of how the student responded, I could have repeatedly offered opportunities for right action and restoration. I could have led with a question instead of an accusation. "Tell me about how you wrote this paper" would have given him opportunity to own up to his plagiarism. Leading with my conclusion ("This is plagiarized") positioned him for self-defense. When he raised his voice at me, I could have stopped him right away and, in a calm voice, invited him to speak to me later when he had calmed down. I could have followed up with him weeks or months later, trying to reestablish a professor-student relationship before he graduated. And, before any of this began, I could have gone out of my way to greet him by name before or after class, making friendly contact before anything contentious was at stake.

Different semester, same opening lines, same outcome (perhaps I need to reconsider the brilliance of that pitch). As a creative assignment about global challenges facing humanity, Gretchen turns in a poster board covered with images of lemmings printed from websites. The metaphor was clever: humans, like lemmings, tend to run *en masse* in dangerous directions. The first text box begins, "Lemmings are small rodents, usually found in or near the Arctic, in tundra biomes."[5] Typing any of about twenty of her sentences into an Internet search engine confirmed one of my bedrock beliefs: if it sounds like Wikipedia, it probably is Wikipedia.

I didn't document the plagiarism exhaustively as I had with Ian's, investing time instead in talking with Gretchen rather than in documenting the extent of her wrong-doing. I asked her to meet me in my office, and as I waited for her, I noticed my heart rate rising, my mouth becoming dry, and my palms getting clammy. I took a deep breath. I set the paper on the table and winced. "Gretchen, can you tell me about how you wrote this?"

She cried. "I know, I know, I copied that stuff off the Internet. It was wrong, and I'm sorry."

I gave her a minute and then asked, "Why did you copy it?"

"I'm so busy," she said. "I had several things due this week, and I didn't start early enough, and then when I did start, I just wanted it to be perfect and everything I wrote seemed lame."

We talked about time management, procrastination, and perfectionism, all pervasive elements of student culture that undermine academic integrity. Because she confessed and apologized, I still gave the assignment a zero, but offered the opportunity to rewrite the paper for half credit. I reassured her that I valued her as a student, that I wouldn't punish her on future papers or tests because of this incident, nor would I hold it against her in any other way.

Inwardly I praised myself for remaining calm, putting the student first, and moving her along in my class.

Gretchen interrupted my self-congratulation with, "Dr. Paris, just one more thing."

"Yes?"

"I just want you to know that this can't affect my overall course grade. I have to get an A in this class."

I stayed calm on the outside, starting over with an explanation of how serious academic integrity is. "It has to affect your overall course grade, Gretchen. That's how serious plagiarism is. Some professors will give you an F in the entire course after a single incident like this."

On the inside I was leaning forward, hands cradling head, exhaling a frustrated "Aaaargh!"

5. Wikipedia, "Lemming."

A few weeks later, I found myself uttering words far worse than "Aaargh!" My boys, then three, three, and one, were napping and I was headed to my bedroom to read *Buddhism for Mothers: A Calm Approach to Caring for Yourself and Your Children*, which I had in hand. I heard rustling, so I opened a door to check on a three-year-old napping boy. He was awake and naked, smiling sheepishly. He had used every item of clothing as a paintbrush to smear his own poop on the walls, carpet, bed, sheets, and blankets. He mostly kept it off his hands that way.

I lost my calm approach to caring for myself and my children, but I didn't lose my temper. I just said, "You need a bath," carried him by the armpits to the bath, and washed him off. Then I climbed into the toilet (a.k.a. his room) and started cleaning. I scraped the big chunks off the carpet and sheets with rags, washed streaks off sheets and blankets in the sink, then threw them in the washing machine with detergent and baking soda, for a fifteen-minute soak, and then a full cycle. I scoured the bedframe and the walls and hauled out the carpet steamer for the carpet. When it looked clean, I crawled around the room nose first, sniffing carpet fibers, bedframe joints, and wall surfaces. Then I scoured it all again.

My son sat against a wall on time-out while I cleaned. When I finished, I asked him why he did it, and he wouldn't speak. I said, "It's OK, honey, I always love you, but this was a very bad thing to do."

He buried his head in my shirt and whispered in a baby voice, "Sorry poo poo."

We struggled through the rest of the day, all three boys acting up in response to the turmoil in the air. After bedtime, I called my mother-in-law to process.

She responded immediately, "Tell me about the shit. What was in it? Was it good for painting? Was there a message written in it?"

I called her because I expected such a response, endowed as she is with equal parts common sense and theatricality. She listened to every last dark brown detail, and offered her best bodily fluid stories from her cache of parenting experience.

The worst part, for me, was the message the boy had written. Though he was too young to write a single letter, much less a word or a sentence, I felt certain I could scrutinize the shit like a psychic reading tea leaves. *I see through the repression of this regime and am protesting the conditions of my confinement. You're a bad mother. I'd like a new one.*

My mother-in-law pointed out the obvious, that I was projecting my fears onto a situation that shouldn't be analyzed with Gramscian theory. After all, philosopher Antonio Gramsci was actually imprisoned under Mussolini's Fascist regime, whereas my boy snuggles up under the quilt I sewed for him in the room painted the blue of his choosing.

She reassured me, "This wasn't something he did to you. It's just something he did." She encouraged me to pay closer attention to the boy than to the mess he made.

"Getting down in the shit with your kids is sacred," she said. "It creates a bond and a love that wasn't there before."

Cheating is the shit of academe. Whether it is students, teachers, or presidents smearing it around the place, it makes a mess. When teachers cheat, we may well lose our jobs or even our careers; there's often little chance for a do-over. When it's our students, however, we can almost always make room for both consequences and restoration.

Unlike my son's curiosity gone awry, cheating almost always conveys a message. For me, and many other teachers I've asked, on first read it seems personal. *I don't like you, don't respect you, don't care about this class. I cheated because it seems easy to get away with in your class.*

Teachers need technique, and they need subject matter expertise, but these matter little without the presence of heart and inspiration. The dictionary tells us that to do something "with heart" means to inspire with confidence, to embolden, to encourage, and to animate. To teach with heart means to be a genuine human presence in the lives of students.

—Sam Intrator[6]

This first read is almost always wrong. The message is something about fear, perfectionism, lack of preparation, personal crisis, apathy, or entitlement. In cheating, the student is saying:

- *I'm overwhelmed.*
- *I'm too busy and I don't know how to handle it.*
- *I don't think I can write well.*

---

6. Intrator, *Stories of the Courage to Teach*, xxxiii.

79

- *I have learning challenges I didn't tell you about.*

- *I put it off until the last minute, panicked, and then cheated.*

- *Writing and studying are hard, and cheating is easy.*

- *I shouldn't have to work so hard.*

- *It's the teacher's job to catch cheating, not my job to not do it.*

- *It doesn't really count if you cheat from your girlfriend's/boyfriend's/best friend's/twin's work.*

These are very different messages and warrant different responses. We miss the sacred when we focus on the stink, whether by ignoring dishonesty so we can steer clear of the mess or by punishing the student without looking at the situation from their vantage point. When we discern the message painted with the shit, teachers can get behind the cover and begin to really educate the student, redirecting them back toward integrity.

9

Survive Crisis

September 11, 2001.

8:44 AM: Flight attendant Amy Sweeney, on American Airlines Flight 11, calls the American Airlines Flight Services Office and reports, "Something is wrong. We are in a rapid descent . . . we are all over the place." A minute later she says, "We are flying low. We are flying very, very low. We are flying way too low." And then, "Oh my God, we are way too low." Her call ends with static.

8:46 AM: Going nearly five hundred mph, American Airlines Flight 11 crashes into the North Tower of the World Trade Center, between floors ninety-three and ninety-nine. The plane plows into the core of the building. People below floor ninety-three begin evacuating, but people above the plane's impact zone are unable to.

8:46 AM to 10:28 AM: At least a hundred people, likely more, jump to their deaths from upper floors of the World Trade Center, trapped by fire and smoke.

8:50 AM: Hijacking begins on American Airlines Flight 77. It soon changes course, turning south over Ohio.

9:03 AM: Going nearly six hundred mph, Flight 175 crashes into the South Tower of the World Trade Center. Millions see it live on television.

9:37 AM: Flight 77 crashes into the Pentagon.

9:59 AM: The South Tower begins to collapse.

10:03 AM: United Airlines Flight 93 crashes near Shanksville, Pennsylvania, after passengers revolt against the hijackers.

10:15 AM: I'm in my office alone with the door cracked open, preparing for class. A colleague rushes down the hall, calling, "There's been a plane crash in New York City!"

My memory blurs. On January 28, 1986, a teacher rushed down my junior high hallway, calling, "The space shuttle crashed!" Their voices sound the same.

I turn on my radio. I have Internet access in my office, but still turn to TV and radio for news. I join people gathered in the hallway talking. I worry, however, that I won't be prepared for class. If I stop my day's work for every tragedy, I figure, nothing would ever get done. I go back to my desk.

10:28 AM: The North Tower begins to collapse.

12:01 PM: Fourteen people, mostly firefighters, climb an intact set of stairs from inside the North Tower and emerge at the top of the rubble.

12:10 PM: One person climbs into her classroom, uncertain. Large-screen televisions are wheeled out to public lounges where lots of people congregated, but classes haven't been cancelled, and won't be. I get my bearings by recalling my job.

I'm a professor. I have class now, and I'm supposed to teach it.

I open with a word of concern and a prayer. Then I stammer, "I guess we'll just keep up with the syllabus," and launched into class as usual.

I taught my night class that evening, too, a decision my husband still finds unforgivable. "You alter your plans. You watch TV. You bear witness," he said.

"But the college didn't cancel class," I insist. "I had to work."

More than a decade later I ask colleagues, "If you were in the classroom on 9/11, what did you do?

A chemistry professor did the same as me, teaching a lab against his better judgment. A former military officer, he was conditioned to do as he was told. Since classes were officially in session, he taught. He turned on a radio in a room behind the lab and dashed back and forth between teaching and checking the news. In retrospect, he says, no one got anything out of that lab session. Everyone would have been better off at home with their families.

Another worried over what his students wanted from him. At first he thought they were looking to him for a sense that the world would go on.

He was reluctant because, "Well, of course, I didn't know if it would." Then he realized what they really wanted was a space to express fear, uncertainty, and mutual support. He gave them that.

Another offered to cancel class, but students wanted to stay. She turned on the classroom television and with her students, watched both towers fall. One student panicked because her mother worked at the Pentagon, but said she'd rather wait for news (which, thankfully, was good) with her classmates than alone in her dorm.

A few teachers tried to connect the tragedy to class concepts. A religion professor tried this, then gave up and turned on the TV at which they all "stared dumbly."

I ask my students the same question, "If you were in class on 9/11, what was it like?"

Most were in upper elementary grades and they stayed in school all day. They had a sense that something was wrong, but they didn't watch TV or listen to the radio with their teachers. They stumbled through the regular school day under the leadership of teachers who were obviously upset, and learned details from their parents after school.

An older student, a high schooler at the time, was in math class. He remembers his teacher as in the same boat as the students: confused, shocked, sad, and afraid. "To see an adult modeling for us what it meant to truly grieve a tragedy during its first few moments, allowing yourself to honestly and earnestly feel what you feel and for that to be okay, to not feel like you had to force some sort of interpretation or articulation of order in the midst of utter chaos—it was honest and right. Something I never forgot."

My class that day, I'm sure, was forgettable, because I did just the opposite. My excessive sense of duty as a worker prevented me from taking in the gravity of the situation. When ordinary things go awry—technology doesn't work, lights are flickering, numerous students come in late—the teacher should keep the class on track and fulfill curricular plans despite distractions. In the midst of extraordinary crisis, the responsibility is the same: to direct the students toward what is most important. The approach, however, is the opposite: instead of staying the course despite distraction, extraordinary crisis calls us to set aside what we had planned to do, and in a manner befitting our context, attend to the more important matter that has burst into our world.

What, in my existence as a person, in my relations with others, in my work as a teacher, is of real concern to me, perhaps of ultimate concern to me? In my teaching I seek to transmit the meanings others have found in their search for truth, and that is good as far as it goes. But as I try to help young people to discover meaning, have I perhaps evaded the question of what life might mean to me? How can I, in my study and my teaching and in the countless topics that engage my thought, find a home within myself?

—Arthur Jersild[1]

On 9/11, students easily found what was most important, and asked the kinds of real and relevant questions teachers long for students to initiate. *Will the world go on? What is happening? Are we safe? How will we respond?*

These are relevant questions for nearly every discipline: math, biology, history, or literature can use real-world crises for application and relevance. This could help students learn something they actually want and need to know, some real stakes beyond the next grade or assessment.

Most of us couldn't simply start teaching about Al Qaeda, terrorism, or the Middle East, because we knew little more than what we heard on the news. We could, however, teach critical thinking, research, investigation, and philosophical reflection skills, applied not to a case study, but to reality as it unfolded.

What would it take to answer these questions? Where does helpful information exist? How can you filter, evaluate, and prioritize sources of information and perspective? What ethical or moral guidelines would help determine what responses are appropriate? What do professionals in [insert field] do that promotes conflict resolution?

We may not be able to avoid, settle, or even interpret crisis, but we wrestle a blessing from it when it shapes our teaching in ways that benefit students: raising the stakes, inspiring learning, and helping prepare students to live and serve meaningfully in the world as it is.

Fortunately, public crises don't disrupt our classrooms every day. Even during ordinary times, however, personal crises challenge our ability to

1. Jersild, *When Teachers Face Themselves*, 4–5.

keep our classes rolling. In *The Skillful Teacher*, Stephen Brookfield compares teaching to white water rafting; periods of calm interspersed with turbulence.

> [A]ll teachers worth their salt regularly ask themselves whether or not they are doing the right thing. Experiencing regular episodes of hesitation, disappointment, and ego-deflation is quite normal. Indeed, the awareness of painful dilemmas in our practice, and the readiness to admit that we are hurting from experiencing these, is an important indicator that we are critically alert . . . . [T]eaching is an experience in which one commonly feels lonely, anxious, alienated, and abused.[2]

In addition to these kinds of professional heartbreaks, we endure personal struggles thatdon't elicit collective response and may not even be visible. We may wish to keep them private and sometimes do, but this isn't always possible.

I easily remember my teachers' problems that spilled over into student view:

- Ms. Hill, my seventh grade math teacher, wore full make-up, hair-sprayed hair, and professional suits every day. She had a foot surgery that required her to wear slippers to class for weeks, and she made awkward jokes about how her slippers compromised her fashion.

- My fifth grade teacher, Mr. Bartelmas, contracted leukemia and had to take a leave that ended with his death. Teachers helped kids write get-well cards, reported updates, and delivered the news of his passing to us during class.

- A third grade teacher at my school divorced and remarried, coming back one fall with a new hyphenated name. Neither divorces nor hyphens were as common as they are now, and students discussed both the divorce and the hyphen at great length.

Death, cancer, divorce, health crises, mental health challenges, break-ups, accidents, and more—none of it waits for three-day weekends or summer breaks. As I learned from personal experience, neither do hangnails.

"Is there a chance I could die in my sleep tonight?" I asked my doctor.

---

2. Brookfield, *Skillful Teacher*, 2.

She replied, "You're a smart lady to worry about that. If I thought you were stupid, I'd admit you. You seem smart enough to watch for emergency symptoms at home."

An infected hangnail on my right ring finger suddenly swelled up so much I couldn't bend my finger. After a day, it bulged with green and yellow pus, and the pain of touching it made me nauseous. A red line began advancing up my arm, a sign that the infection had entered deeper tissue and was headed for my heart. I went to the doctor, bringing along a stack of student essays that needed to be graded.

The doctor could lance it and prescribe antibiotics, or I could be admitted for hospital staff to do the same, with the added benefit of overnight supervision. That's when I asked about the possibility of death. If the infection might zap my heart, I'd rather be admitted. If not, I'd rather be at home where at least I'd have the chance to get to work the next day.

If death were coming, she said, I'd first have chills and fever, but even then there'd be enough time to get to the hospital, and even if I got there slowly, amputation of my finger or hand could still save my life. Reassured by the number of steps between my current condition and death, I let her treat the wound. She said, "You're going to feel this," and sawed with a scalpel around the entire cuticle to release blood and pus. I distracted myself by reading student papers, trying to memorize the comments I'd need to go back and make once I could use my right hand again. I headed home with a clean wound and megadoses of two antibiotics.

The doctor told me to rest for a day, but I agonized over canceling class. I don't have graduate students to fill in for me, nor did I want to ask a colleague to substitute on such short notice. There were only two class sessions left before Thanksgiving break, and I didn't want to carry November's material over into December.

I canceled, undoubtedly the right choice for my health, but what would it mean for the class? I determined to keep up, so next class session I taught all the material, twice as fast. Cramming two lectures and two active learning exercises into one period was impossible, and I knew it. I should have done what my doctor did: inspect the situation with intelligence and dispassion, acknowledge the pain, and start cutting.

I told a colleague about my day and he laughed. "Ah, the old 'double the speed, double the coverage' technique!" He had fallen for it many times himself. It's what my former colleague Dan Taylor calls the "myth of coverage." Dan says teachers seem to believe that if they utter all the words related to a topic, or assign all the best reading on the topic, then the topic has been covered. These techniques stem from a deeper fallacy, perhaps easiest to believe at the college level, that we teach subjects, not students. When teachers attempt to cover a topic, we often bury it instead. When we focus on subjects instead of students, a sick day seems to derail our carefully planned syllabus. When we focus instead on uncovering the topic, revealing enough of it, and in such a way as to inspire students' interest and competent engagement, then learning is happening.[3]

It's hard, maybe impossible, to reflect productively on teaching and learning when extreme stress triggers a fight-or-flight response. I've tried both flight and fight: my response to 9/11 was a flight response. *I can't stop for every tragedy. I'll just carry on as usual until someone tells me to do otherwise.* In response to my hangnail, I chose to fight. *I'll just teach harder, faster! This won't slow down my class.*

The fight-or-flight response is useful in a pinch, but when crisis is the tenor of everyday life, as it is in many educational settings today, a broader repertoire of responses is needed. We may not always be able to see it in the moment, but on reflection we can observe the fight-or-flight response as it arises, and rather than follow it impulsively, make a choice.

Easier said than done: the word *crisis* denotes an unstable, unpredictable, dangerous time that doesn't yield to our attempts to shape it. Crisis seems to be the norm for American education, for at least the last very long while. Some say this is manufactured, pointing to the ways in which the careers of politicians, authors, and administrators expand along with the inflation of whatever crisis they proclaim. Additionally, today's media—social media, as well as reality shows—thrive in their extremeness. Schools and teachers aren't nearly as exciting as legal, criminal, hospital, or political drama, but at least we've got crisis.

Crises may be manufactured, at least to some extent and some of the time, but today's "crisis in education" certainly seems real to me. In higher education, many full-time and tenured faculty have frozen or reduced salaries and benefits, that is, if their departments, programs, and jobs haven't been cut. Most faculty are adjunct, teaching numerous classes per year, sometimes for numerous universities, with little hope for benefits, long-term contracts, or sustainable wages. My professor friends who are out of work despair of getting a toehold in the academy, turning instead to

---

3. See Palmer, *To Know as We Are Known.*

entry-level work in an unrelated field or hourly work in the service industry. Friends who do have work are overloaded, stressed, and worry about the fate of their disciplines, their programs, and even their universities. In K–12 I hear teachers despair about the demands of standardized testing, competition over scores, and the devaluing of their skills and expertise. A friend attended her back-to-school teacher's retreat in late August and came away saying, "That wasn't a retreat. It had the feel of a funeral—everyone's depressed and it's all going to hell."

[T]he critical and dynamic view of the world strives to unveil reality, unmask its mythicization, and achieve a full realization of the human task: the permanent transformation of reality in favor of the liberation of people.

—PAULO FREIRE[4]

We teach in a climate of crisis, and all of us alive today were educated in the same. In the 1980s, the crisis was the shoddiness of American education. President Reagan's "A Nation at Risk" report warned,

> Our once unchallenged preeminence in commerce, industry, science, and technological innovation is being overtaken by competitors throughout the world . . . . We report to the American people that while we can take justifiable pride in what our schools and colleges have historically accomplished and contributed to the United States and the well-being of its people, the educational foundations of our society are presently being eroded by a rising tide of mediocrity that threatens our very future as a Nation and a people.[5]

Before this, Neil Postman warned that 1960s education was irrelevant and outdated, confusing schooling with educating, and failing to prepare citizens for a world of constant change. In making his case, he quotes James Agee's description of 1930s education in Alabama, concluding, "with few exceptions . . . , Agee's condemnation of the school curriculum circa 1936 *is entirely applicable to the present day.* In plain truth, what passes for a curriculum in today's schools is little else but a strategy of distraction, as it was

---

4. Freire, *Pedagogy of the Oppressed*, 83.
5. "A Nation at Risk."

in Alabama in 1936. It is largely designed to *keep* students from knowing themselves and their environment in any realistic sense . . . ."[6]

In 1947, Robert Ulich, professor of the history and philosophy of education, explained that education and its associated civilization must be connected in mutual nourishment, and "when the contact is cut they are sick and a crisis occurs. We live now in such a crisis."[7]

Even Martin Luther, in sixteenth-century Germany, warned, "the schools are deteriorating throughout Germany. The universities are becoming weak, the monasteries are declining . . . . Yea, what have men learned hitherto in the universities and monasteries, except to be asses and blockheads?"[8]

Neil Postman and Charles Weingartner say human survival is central to the work of education. Their vision of good education "develops in youth a competence in applying the best available strategies for survival in a world filled with unprecedented troubles, uncertainties, and opportunities. Our task, then, is to make these strategies for survival visible and explicit in the hope that someone somewhere will act on them."[9]

By the root meanings of the words, teachers should *show* or *point out*. Professors should *publically declare*. Educators should *bring out*, or *lead forth*. Whether we are showing mathematical proofs, pointing out the best nursing practices, or leading forth student teachers into elementary schools, our work makes visible strategies for human survival, including survival of human bodies, and intellect and spirit as well.

We must do more than teach and promote survival, of course: we ourselves must survive the inner, interpersonal, and institutional crises that inevitably come our way. Stephen Brookfield warns, "[I]f you do burn out, get fired, become crucified, sacrifice your position fruitlessly, or are consumed by pessimism about the limits of your influence, then you are no good to anyone, least of all to your students. So paying attention to your survival as a teacher is not a narcissistic conceit; it is a fundamental necessity that you owe to yourself and to your students."[10]

6. Postman and Weingartner, *Teaching as a Subversive Activity*, 47.

7. Ulich, *Three Thousand Years*, v.

8. Ibid., 221.

9. Postman and Weingartner, *Teaching as a Subversive Activity*, xv.

10. Brookfield, *Skillful Teacher*, 4.

Crisis on the scale of 9/11 doesn't happen every day, thankfully, but one of the most important learning objectives applicable to all teachers is delivered not by school boards, testing agencies, or general education committees. Reality itself challenges us to survive, to live and teach and learn well in circumstances of rapid change, resource deprivation, and extreme catastrophe, both rhetorical and real.

In addition to instructing students, we can let them see us being instructed by the world, as it unfolds in real time. In addition to knowing our subject, we need to discern when and how to let students see our not knowing. And while we certainly must direct the semester from beginning to end, we need not control it or micromanage it. Sometimes, staring dumbly is the best pedagogy.

Nurturing our inner lives—cultivating attentiveness, depth, joy, and meaning—will surely benefit teachers' responses to crisis. Earlier I described spirituality as something like *a!ia*, the Ju/'hoansi word for a mysterious presence that is activated by their healing dances. Everyone participates in a dance, traditionally an all-night ceremony that involves visiting, resting, dancing, and healing. The ritual prompts healers to go into a trance, a dangerous state in which they may throw themselves on fire or run out into the wild unprotected. During the trance, *a!ia* boils up in the healer's stomach, bubbling out through his arms and fingers as healing energy that can draw out sickness from others. The healing dance would be performed weekly, or even more often, even during ordinary times, and the presumption was that everyone always needed healing, most often from daily wounds such as jealousy, bickering, or disappointment.

When healers go into a trance, they die. The healer willingly faces his fear of death, moving past it into an altered state of being. When I teach Ju/'hoansi ritual in anthropology classes, students don't recognize this as death because they are conditioned by Western views of death as permanent and marked by absence of brain activity. They easily recognize parallels in their own experience, however: a man who lifts a vehicle to free a person trapped beneath it, the runner's "wall," or certain charismatic spiritual experiences. In extreme situations, people sense immanent limits, but press forward and emerge stronger, sometimes even as heroes.

We might imagine spirituality to be about happiness and serenity, but that isn't even the half of it. A spiritual life, or a soulful life, is less about niceness, pleasantry, or even goodness, and more about depth and wholeness.

Whether we call it God or the gods, spirit or spirits, *a!ia* or something else, depth of spirit strengthens us to live through the full range of human experience, which includes death, darkness, annihilation and trauma, both in our unrealized fears and in reality. Ju/'hoansi healers go forward toward death because they trust that on the other side is healing power that will benefit their community. This trust is grounded in experience: they've seen others cross back and forth between death and life, between sickness and health, between normal times and crisis.[11]

Living with spirit isn't merely a magic trick to pull out of one's sleeve in an emergency: it may be expressed in particularly intense ways in certain circumstances, but it changes us in more ordinary ways as well. In recounting her life story, a Ju/'hoansi woman named !Nisa describes times of hardship, deprivation, and loss, concluding that the best times of her life when she and her family were "just living."[12] A Zen perspective might encourage "just living," especially with respect to crisis. In addressing terrorism and world violence, Thich Nhat Hanh advises people to calm down, look with deep understanding, and act from that understanding. Just breathe, just look, just understand, just live. "Every bit of our understanding, compassion, and peace is useful; it is gold . . . . It is not about 'doing' something, it's about 'being' something—being peace, being hope, being solid—every action will come out of that, because peace, stability, and freedom always seek a way to express themselves in action."[13]

When our three boys were all under the age of two, I used to complain that we should be happier; in fact, we should be thriving. None of us ever slept through the night, and it seemed someone was always catching a virus that got passed around via sneezes, fevers, or vomit. Nonetheless, I insisted, we have these beautiful babies, and we should be happy! My husband said, "Look, I think you need to lower your standards. We just need to survive." Having a house full with three healthy babies was a crisis of sorts, an extreme and unusual time that warranted a change of schedule, change of plans, and change of standards.

He was right, except for the notion that focusing on survival would be a lowering of standards. The days when I truly did focus on survival— *feed the babies, change the babies, get some sleep*—were the happiest days,

11. Katz, Biesele, and St. Denis, *Healing Makes Our Hearts Happy.*
12. Shostak, *Nisa.*
13. Hanh and Neumann, *Calming the Fearful Mind,* 41.

because the rumination was quieted. Striving for more—*shouldn't I be happier?*—was actually the lower standard.

The spiritual practice is to survive crisis with as much of our personal and collective humanity intact as possible. This is humanity's ongoing work in response to 9/11, a global tangle of concerns related to human security that is ongoing and seemingly permanent. This is our work with respect to the physical well-being of students and teachers in schools threatened by gun violence. This is our work in our own personal crises, the problems of our specific schools, and the challenges of our profession.

We can notice our instinctual responses to fear (fight, flee, or avoid), which is to honor fear as a survival instinct. Then, we must calm down enough to expand the range of options for response. These options cannot be known in advance, but we can trust they will flow from our calm understanding.

10

Be True to Your School

So be true to your school now
Just like you would to your girl or guy
Be true to your school now
And let your colors fly
Be true to your school

Rah rah rah be true to your school
Rah rah rah be true to your school
Rah rah rah be true to your school
Rah rah rah be true to your school

—THE BEACH BOYS

Teachers often carry lofty, personified, even romanticized expectations toward our schools. As in a life partnership, we begin with high expectations and a good measure of happiness. We give ourselves over to our schools: spend personal funds on school supplies, carry student papers around with us, and plan curriculum during our kids' sporting events. Some even receive awards for "going above and beyond" or "giving one hundred and ten percent"; in short, giving more than we've contracted to give. We hope to be valued, understood, respected—even loved—by our school.

One way or another, the honeymoon ends. It may turn lackluster, both you and the school sticking with it for the sake of the kids. Or it may turn into an abusive relationship in which you keep your head down and stays out of the school's way when it comes at you drunk and angry. Or a teacher may career toward despair, spending years assessing whether or not he's being abused, talking endlessly with friends and therapists about whether to stay, try to change the situation, or leave. Even though we know a school isn't a person, in relation to our school we experience the emotions of human relationships: betrayal, punishment, shame, and fear. Over time, a teacher may come to terms with the nature of the relationship and its limits and benefits for the long haul. This could be a sullen stalemate, mutual sadism, or maybe something surprisingly enduring and mutually beneficial.

Catchy as the song is, The Beach Boys' lyrics don't ring literally true: school spirit is not *just like* being true to one's lover. I've said, and heard, many comments that personify institutions, such as these:

- *Would the college get mad at me if I published this?*

- *The university said these hard financial times are our "new normal."*

- *The school decided to suspend those athletes even though they'll miss a big game.*

But the school can't get mad, make decisions, or say anything, because the school is not a person. What exactly is "the school" or "the college"? I've pressed hard at times to figure out just who might get mad, or just who made a decision, to trace back the line of responsibility to an actual human agent, and it is often impossible. "The school" isn't exactly the principal, school board, or board of regents, though the individuals who fill these roles can sometimes speak for, make decisions on behalf of, or even symbolize, the school. It doesn't have an office or an email address, but somehow the institution has a life of its own, one that relates very closely to the life of each teacher.

Should The Beach Boys ever consult a social scientist, I might say the bond between teacher and school is like a relationship, except when it's not. It is not a partnership between equals. We're not in it together until one of us dies, as in a marriage. Unless the school closes, the employee will die first, and it may well be the institution that does you in. No matter how noble its purpose or how fair its policies, an institution is not a person: it cannot love you back.

Just what might it mean, then, to be true to your school?

Relational metaphors quickly reach their limits because institutions are not persons, yet it's hard to find better ones. In our society, we personify things and commodify people. We speak of *loving, lusting after,* even *to die for* a car, a house, or just plain money. Corporations are legal persons and though they have no mouths, their free speech is protected. In pointed contrast, actual people are bought and sold for labor and for sex. And in everyday ways, we commodify our faces, bodies, and identities when we craft them for others' consumption. No wonder, then, it's hard to define what a person is in relation to a system or an institution, a teacher in relation to her school. This may be vital, however, for our work as teachers, no matter our subject: what is a person, and what is a thing? How can we see clearly, and live well, in a world that confuses the two?

Many workplace metaphors are extremely negative: the gulag, Big Brother, the Death Star, the looney bin, and _____ holes, the blank filled with words related to excrement, hell, or filth. Employees describe themselves as rats in a cage, cogs in a machine, hamsters on a wheel, or human beings trapped in holes. Organizational leaders may be diabolical kings or queens, totalitarian despots, inmates running the asylum, or animals running the zoo.

Perhaps each teacher needs a working metaphor, one that helps us picture our work as more than grim duty, and ourselves as more than victims or martyrs. A school administrator encouraged teachers to do as he does, pause every five years or so and reflect on what he is doing, and why. He said, "This might be misunderstood as a personal crisis or a problem, but really, it's not a problem to ask, 'what am I doing? is this for me? what is my purpose?' For some, the work no longer fits them, and they need to move on. For others, they need to pause, reflect, and rediscover the source of their energy."

I teach in a variety of contexts, with metaphors suited to each. When I teach Sunday school, I'm a pinch hitter, a substitute when others are absent. When I teach community education, I'm a breath of fresh air. I blow in, do my thing for five sessions, and blow back out. At the first college where I taught, I saw myself first as an alumna, and my employer as my alma mater, because it was. The metaphor served me well at that college, where a history of healthy and meaningful relationships made it safe for more personal investment.

It's much more difficult to find working metaphors when a school is sick, your work area is dysfunctional, or, for any number of reasons, the environment isn't safe. Mary Rose O'Reilley worked for years in a dysfunctional English department, and searched for a metaphor that would keep her open to forgiveness and to the possibility of a better future. She came to see it as a "school for love."[1] Rather than a problem, a drain, or a pit of despair, she came to see her workplace as a setting for her own education.

The passion that accompanies our attention to subjects, issues, and children is not just something we offer our students. It is also a gift we grant ourselves: a way of honoring our life's work, our profession. It says: "I know why I am devoting this life I've got to these children."

—Robert Fried,[2] *The Passionate Teacher*

I've been unable to think of a good metaphor myself, until I saw a student's wedding photos that went viral after the husband posted them online.[3] Lynette and Cory were married in Zimbabwe (she is from Zimbabwe, and he is from the United States). Photos show them riding elephants to their outdoor wedding site, dismounting, and then walking down the aisle. In one photo, Lynette and Cory are kissing: she has one hand wrapped around his neck, the other hand holding a bright orange bouquet. Two elephants stand behind them, one tusk very close to Cory's head. The photos went viral because of the beautiful location, but also because of their juxtapositions. Absorbed in a kiss, with an elephant tusk inches from your head. Pristinely dressed up, in the outdoors. Vulnerable and tender, with large carnivores close at hand.

That's my metaphor: my school is the elephant that carries me. The elephant's power can be breathtaking, when I'm lifted up to heights I could never reach on my own. When the elephant and I move in tandem, exciting adventures result. Its power can also be threatening, even crushing. At my best, I'm happy as a wedding guest, moved to vulnerability and tenderness,

1. O'Reilley, *Garden at Night*, 67.

2. Fried, *Passionate Teacher*, 19.

3. "African Wedding."

hopeful that everyone will move forward toward a happy future. The elephant tusk is always inches from my head, however, and I'm often uncertain why it's there or what it's about to do.

Mary Rose O'Reilley is writing as an English teacher, lover of metaphors. In disciplines such as mine, analysis of institutions is central to our work as social scientists. In this view, we step into the position of "teacher" because the school institutionalizes this role, as well as the role of student. We rely on schools to give us classrooms, electricity, utilities, security, parking lots, health insurance, retirement, and paychecks. Yet when teachers join administration, working on behalf of the institution and even becoming a symbol of it to the public, teachers may see this as buying in or selling out. At my college, when professors become administrators, they often joke that they've "crossed over to the dark side."

Political scientist Hugh Heclo posits that modern life predisposes us to distrust institutions. Modern ideas of individual rights, happiness, and autonomy encourage the notion that an institutionally unencumbered self would be the happiest one. Furthermore, in recent decades and centuries and epochs, corruption and abuses of power by institutional leaders have confirmed these suspicions. Heclo lists five pages of shady political and legal events spanning from 1958 through the early 2000s, concluding that everyone alive today has good reason for distrust.

We may not actively distrust, or think about it explicitly, but there is a "fixed slant in our frame of reference" that leans against institutions.[4] In left-leaning disciplines such as mine, it seems more intelligent and critical—*interesting*, as we academics like to say—to see institutions as socially constructed regimes of power that are, first and foremost, devoted to self-preservation. But from what vantage point do we launch such a critique? The teenager can only insult her parents from within the household on which her livelihood depends. Likewise, we demand freedom and autonomy from a position of profound dependence on the very institutions we critique, a stance that generates bitterness and acrimony. As Heclo explains, "To live in our times is to be thoroughly dependent on the competence and dutifulness of strangers in far-flung institutional settings, people with whom we have never contracted, much less really know. Institutions can

---

4. Heclo, *On Thinking Institutionally.*

evoke our distrust because we need them so much. Resentment is the price self-respect extracts for such dependence."[5]

Distrust won't likely go away: it is well-deserved and deeply embedded in the logic of modernity. Overidentification will also continue. Those rewarded by institutions will merge their personal identities with the institution, working round the clock and round the year, becoming hypersensitive or paranoid about both personal and institutional criticism, because they seem to be one and the same. Overidentification and distrust, then, feed one another, to everyone's detriment.

Heclo encourages a move from thinking about institutions to thinking institutionally, a learned skill that promises to improve our lives, given our inescapable dependence on institutions. "We may well distrust institutionalized organizations and those people who would abuse their power. But we can still value the humane purposes of 'good' institutions, especially the superintending institutions of law and government that all the others depend on. We can work at thinking and acting institutionally in the business of daily life."[6]

He considers this an appreciative stance, though overidentifiers may think it less than loyal, and distrusters may think it selling out. I find it intriguing and potentially productive, having spent much of my career responding to institutions either as an adolescent, distancing myself from institutional flaws in immature and unproductive ways, or as a lover, expecting an unrealistic degree of affection and inclusion.

In a seminar, I hear one teacher express simple gratitude, "Teaching is a sweet gig. We get to read, write, and think, and bring students along for the ride."

Another, "And even better, the school pays me to read, think, and write ideas that are critical even of them!"

The first is simple enthusiasm; the second, appropriate institutionalism. Toward her school she is both appreciative and critical, dutiful without mindless loyalty.

Imagine Heclo's political advice applied to an educational setting, being true to your school by thinking and acting along with it, and from the stance of an appreciative insider. Particular organizations, a particular school, for instance, are supposed to advance institutional ends, the higher purpose or

5. Ibid., 37.
6. Ibid., 183.

point of coherence for local organizations. The government should advance social stability, law should preserve order, and education should promote people's ability to learn and live well. When your daily work harmonizes with your school, and with the greater purpose of education, this may be a pleasant elephant ride, but this is not always the case.

When organizations stray from their purpose, or even actively work against it, people working within them face difficult choices. A school may prefer robotic loyalty over discerning engagement, sometimes even elevating loyalty to a form of morality. This puts anyone with intelligence and conscience in a hard spot, resulting in "anguishing choices to be made in matters of personal duty and organizational loyalty . . . . When does the whistle-blower blow too quickly or too often? What line will tell us that a police force, military unit, or teachers' union has gone too far in protecting their own? . . . Answers to such questions have to be sought by consulting the larger purposes of any institution for genuine human well-being."[7]

Sometimes blowing the whistle, even getting yourself fired, is a powerful move that results in change. Other times it's just immature and fruitless. I read a story about a public school teacher who didn't believe in standardized testing, so on the days preceding an important test, he'd do something the principal would be sure to see, like march the students outside and have them re-enact a history lesson he thought was more important. He was fired at the end of his first year, the only visible result being the scathing blog post he published about his experience, read by only a few people outside his immediate family.

In contrast, Jennifer Haselberger spoke out against her employer in a way that resulted in both her termination and meaningful change. A devout Catholic, Haselberger spent years earning a law degree, then studied canon law in order to serve the church as a canon lawyer. In 2008 she began serving as chancellor of canonical affairs for the St. Paul-Minneapolis archdiocese. She discovered unreported allegations of clergy sex abuse and gaps in investigations. She raised the issues internally for several years, and after five years resigned from her position, alerting the police and media to the abuse allegations. She said she "found it impossible to continue in her position knowing such gaffes existed and that her efforts to rectify them had proved futile."[8]

7. Ibid., 91.

8. Roewe, "Former Minnesota."

She broke loyalty with a particular organization—her archdiocese and employer—out of duty to possible victims, but also out of loyalty to the institution, the church. She said she remembered a phrase she heard as an undergraduate at St. Catherine University, a Catholic school in Minnesota, "Be loving critics and critical lovers of the institutional church."[9] By calling a corrupt organization back to its true institutional purpose, or at least calling out the fact that it is failing to listen to such a call, Haselberger acted as a loving critic, expressing a loyalty more true than the false morality of group loyalty, and more productive than adolescent complaining.

More often, thinking and acting institutionally in everyday life involves problems that annoy, distract, and discourage, but that don't rise to the level of whistle-blowing, leaving, or even considering leaving. The elephant doesn't attack; it farts.

Whether problems are great or small, the response is similar. First, look deeply at the nature of the institution, its structure, the flow of power through it, its effect on those who take certain roles within it, and its effect on the ethos of the entire school. Seeing that, and seeing our own position and role, and how we are shaped by the flow of power, puts us in position to look and act with compassion toward ourselves, our students, our colleagues, leaders, and even the institution itself.

From a deep understanding, we can cheer our schools on, or call them back toward their highest purpose. Paulo Freire calls this "bearing witness," a "constant, humble and courageous witness emerging from cooperation in a shared effort."[10] Witness varies with cultural context, but has some universal dimensions:

> *Consistency* between words and actions; *boldness* which urges the witnesses to confront existence as a permanent risk; *radicalization* (not sectarianism) leading both the witnesses and the ones receiving that witness to increasing action; *courage to love* (which, far from being accommodation to an unjust world, is rather the transformation of that world on behalf of the increasing liberation of humankind); and *faith* in the people, since it is to them that witness is made . . . .[11]

9. Browning, "Archdiocese Insider."

10. Freire, *Pedagogy of the Oppressed*, 157.

11. Ibid.

Witness can be as small as my shop teacher in high school administering the Comprehensive Tests of Basic Skills with a friendly growl, "Here's your CTBS. Remember kids, it's heavy on the BS." It was sarcastic and perhaps contrary to his contract, but his words reminded us that he saw us as more than test-taking automatons. Witness can be as big as Freire's work in improving basic literacy pedagogy and access for Brazilian peasants, or as big as Jennifer Haselberger's whistle-blowing that has called forward more abuse survivors, and that is making noise heard even in Rome. Witness can be collective action within an institution, either committing to work for change through existing channels, or agitating for systemic change with strategies that are firm but compassionate in both intent and implementation. It can be as simple as going to work with a good attitude, being hopeful about the possibility of positive changes within our schools, and working on committees and taskforces with genuinely positive effort. It may be as humble as retreating for a time of self-preservation and restoration after a discouraging episode.

Some religious leaders asked Jesus, "Should the Jews pay their taxes?" They were presenting a Catch-22: if Jesus said no, he would honor the revolutionary spirit of Jews who hated Roman oppression, but would show himself to be a traitor to Rome. If he said yes, he would show himself to be a sell-out.

Jesus held up a coin and asked, "Whose image is on this coin?"

"Ceasar's," someone replied.

Jesus said, "Give back to Caesar what is Caesar's, and to God what is God's."

Giving yourself over entirely to a job or a vocation, no matter how noble—*I am yours, all my time and energy, my dreams for meaningful productivity, my desire to exercise my gifts and change the world*—is giving away something sacred. It makes us available to abuse; that is, overwork, punishment and shame, or an inability to ever set the work down. And we may respond to abuse by taking more of it, living in unproductive stalemate, or by languishing as victims or martyrs.

The metaphor isn't mean-spirited; in fact, it works as a framework for a happy marriage, too. My husband deserves my respect, my partnership, my effort and investment on a daily basis, but there are limits to what I give over to even my most intimate life partnership. If I give my husband my self-esteem, autonomy, and bodily authority, I've given too much to Caesar. Giving yourself over entirely isn't love, it's self-annihilation.

Being true to a lover, to a cause, or to a school means giving over a rightful portion of your heart, energy, and time. To serve with honesty, respect and dignity, but not unquestioning loyalty, and not infinite time and energy. To distrust, but value and contribute. To hold back what is sacred so that, in the long run, there will be something left of you, and something left to give.

11

Fall in Love

If I speak in the tongues of mortals and of angels, but do not
have love, I am a noisy gong or a clanging cymbal. And if I have
prophetic powers, and understand all mysteries and all knowledge,
and if I have all faith, so as to remove mountains, but do not have
love, I am nothing.

—1 Cor 13:1–2 (NRSV)

I look back over my year's high-low journal and see the word "love" used
for only two reasons: being in class, and enjoyment of students, both
individuals and students in general:

- *First day of class. I loved it.*

- *My student is so mentally ill, I fear she will be homeless or dead someday. I love talking with her, though, and was glad she came by today.*

- *Did my best today—loved it.*

I tell this story in a seminar for teacher development, where the topic
is cultivating the teacher's inner life. Pushback is immediate. One teacher
audibly harrumphed. "Uh, maybe this is for advanced teachers, and I'll try

it in five or ten years. I'd settle for just liking my students. For me, love doesn't come into the workplace."

Another said, "Teaching is a job. Just go do your job. Students don't need someone to love. They need a teacher."

Someone else asked the "just a job" guy, "Well, don't you think you should care for students? Isn't *care* and *regard* part of what we're supposed to do?"

He agreed, but he wasn't going to have warm fuzzies or soft-heartedness with his students, and for him, that's what *love* connoted. The harrumpher said she was questioning whether or not teaching was for her. She couldn't imagine loving students, because she really didn't even like them.

Another bemoaned, "Love is at odds with everything I'm evaluated on. We need to get students in position to make a living, to be richer for having been here. Existential wealth—richness of heart, bounty of perspective, or love—seems an unaffordable luxury. They need jobs."

A final critic said he'd just recently heard big values like "unity" and "trust" used to cover over systemic racism and power abuses at his school. There had been an incident of violence, and the administration responded with a "rally for unity" that, to his ear, sounded like covering over the real and ongoing problems that had contributed to the violence. *Love* is just one more big value that can be used to manipulate people.

Love is risky, both in word and deed. Common uses of the word trivialize, privatize, soften, and sexualize it. Love in the workplace, especially between "providers" and "clients," a model that describes the teacher role, connotes harassment and abuse and lawsuits. The prospect of love raises challenging questions.

- Is love just an invitation to bad boundaries, favoritism, or even abuse?

- Is love a manipulative trick meant to domesticate our critical insight?

- Is love an unaffordable luxury, given today's pressures to take tests, build skills, and make money?

- Should love just stay at home, or in the movies?

- Does love mean softened standards?

- How can we show love to repellant students?

These questions can and should be answered. Love is a risk worth taking, because the alternative—not loving—is risky in its own way. As we find boundaries, consider difficult cases, and develop context-appropriate definitions of and expressions of love, our inner life, including the passion that got us into teaching in the first place, comes into harmony with the work we do. Love unifies a teacher's heart with her work and bonds teachers and students together for productive, whole-hearted, life-changing learning. Teacher educator William Proefriedt challenges new teachers: "Your task is to define and develop a form of loving which will enable you to preserve your central role as teacher; that is, the fostering of the student's ability to evaluate the world around him and to make significant choices concerning it."[1]

> A knowledge that springs from love will implicate us in the web of life; it will wrap the knower and the known in compassion, in a bond of awesome responsibility as well as transforming joy; it will call us to involvement, mutuality, accountability.
>
> —PARKER PALMER[2]

First Corinthians 13 is often read at weddings, but it applies well to teaching. Our job is to speak, to muse about the future, and to ponder mysteries and gather knowledge, but if we do this without love, we are nothing more than a clanging cymbal. My kids' first grade teacher got students' attention with responsive clapping, SLOW-SLOW-QUICK-QUICK-QUICK. Her claps were invitations, and the kids accepted. She was a loving teacher, bringing the kids along with age-appropriate enticements like claps, songs, and puppets. In contrast, Ms. Foster, one of my junior high teachers, achieved the same surface purpose, getting students' attention, by yelling and once even throwing a dictionary at a kid. Both teachers knew their subjects and taught dutifully, but there was a vast difference between the one who loved and the one who didn't, and a vast difference in what students learned.

Many of my teachers inspired me to love them. In eighth grade, my best friend Veda and I loved Mr. Halvorson, joining the yearbook staff because he asked us to. He taught us to design and make a yearbook, including photography and writing. He told our parents we were great students. At

1. Proefriedt, *Teacher You Choose to Be*, 60.
2. Palmer, *To Know as We Are Known*, 9.

the time, we giggled over how much we liked his Bill Cosby sweaters and his feathered hair, but in retrospect, I see that we were thriving as students under his mentorship. In college I fell for professor after professor. I was old enough to laugh at myself for these crushes, but still young enough to throw my heart into them. Dr. Nye called herself a feminist (a word I knew as an insult, not a self-identification), and tossed in a swear word or two into lectures about injustice. She also wore lipstick and high heels, and when we challenged her feminism on that point, she laughed and said she likes for her husband to think she's pretty. Dr. Stone captivated me from the first day of college when I joined his Introduction to Philosophy class. I'd just happen to walk by his office during office hours, ask about Kierkegaard's existentialism or Nietzsche's purpose in claiming "God is dead," then sit back and listen.

I really thought I was in love with them, all of them, male or female, young or old, attractive or not. As a first-year college student, I developed a grand theory of love that stated attraction is ultimately unified. Physical, intellectual, spiritual, sexual, and emotional attraction all converge in the apex of true love. By 2:00 AM, exhausted from socializing and eating sugar, my friends would see the brilliance of my theory. The theory doesn't work well beyond its original context, but it wasn't half bad there, lying on my back in a dorm room admiring the poster of Andre Agassi tacked to the ceiling, listening to U2, and writing metatheories with lavender sparkly gel pen in my journal.

From my vantage point now, married eighteen years to a man with whom I've made a family and a life, I look back at those teacher crushes as just that—bursts of genuine admiration bolstered by free-ranging adolescent sexual energy. With my husband, I want to make things: meals, a home, love, babies, and plans. I want to make a life with him. With my teachers, I just wanted to have, not to make. I wanted to have a sense that my life could be as amazing as theirs. I wanted to have a peek at their libraries, their course notes, and the family photos on their desks. I wanted to have a chance to pretend I was them. One time, when Dr. Stone left his office briefly, I had a friend take a picture of me sitting behind his desk, so I could see what I might look like as a professor.

My instinct to get close to teachers I loved was sound. What I really wanted was to burrow into the possibilities that their lives held open to me, and beg, borrow or steal as much as I could for my own future. The giggling over a professor's hairstyle, the ruminating about her love life, or the inspection of his comments on my essay as perhaps a coded message of undying devotion were just age-appropriate froth that covered the surface of something purely delicious, the true love of a student for her teacher.

I love my students, too. When I was younger, I felt like a camp counselor, fully engaged with them in an adventure in which I carried leadership responsibility. Now that I'm twice their age, my love is more maternal.

The naming of the world, which is an act of creation and re-creation, is not possible if it is not infused with love. Love is at the same time the foundation of dialogue and the dialogue itself . . . . If I do not love the world—if I do not love life—if I do not love people—I cannot enter into dialogue.

—PAULO FREIRE[3]

Martin approaches me after the first day of class, formal as can be. "Dr. Paris, I've made a personal commitment to do better this year. I am declaring this intention to each of my professors in hopes that it will help me stick to my commitment." Then he relaxed and smiled, "I mean, I'm not asking you to be my mother or anything, but I won't mind if you ask me whether I'm keeping up with the reading."

Paulo Freire would encourage me not to be Martin's "mother or anything." He warns against parental love as a metaphor for the affection between teacher and student, even hinting that teachers who rely on this metaphor may only be pretending to teach. In his view, when teachers think of themselves as parents, they become domesticated. Instead of radicalizing their students, they coddle them. Instead of struggling against injustice with a clear and critical eye, teachers turn soft as the teddy bears they give to their own children.[4] Proefriedt warns against love that turns manipulative, particularly when teachers think they know the values and conclusions students ought to reach, and use affection to save students from themselves, reducing their autonomy in making decisions for themselves.[5]

3. Freire, *Pedagogy of the Oppressed*, 70–71.
4. Freire, *Teachers as Cultural Workers*, 15.
5. Proefriedt, *Teacher You Choose to Be*, 57.

I get that, and add to it a feminist critique of teacher as mother. Professional women should not be expected to bring nurture, warmth, and softened standards simply because of their gender, or even because they may be mothers. Students shouldn't expect that a professor's concern for them will translate into an undeserved A in a course, the way a mother's heart may compel her to soften her child's well-deserved punishment. Students shouldn't be infantilized, and teachers shouldn't be de-professionalized.

Certainly my love for them is not maternal, insofar as mothers are domestic servants to their children. I don't want to do their laundry, clean up after them, or persuade them to wash their armpits. I don't want to coddle them, but then, I don't coddle my own children. I hope to radicalize my sons just like my students, honing their "crap detectors" so they can distinguish truth from lies and justice from oppression, and do something purposeful and helpful with their lives.[6] I hold them—students and sons, both—to high standards, sometimes offering encouragement and help and sometimes withholding assistance so they can struggle toward independence. And whether they succeed or fail, even when failure is their own fault, I love them. I love my boys with kisses and sweet talk, and my students with a pat on the arm and casual phrases—*Hey, great job!*—or focused conversation, but it's the same kind of love: a heart-felt concern for their well-being and esteem that is unaltered by their success or failure. Raymond Blakney, former President of Olivet College in Michigan, writes,

> a great teacher is a moral force in the classroom as elsewhere, but that suggests the unlovely picture of a stern disciplinarian. It is probably sufficient to say that the unsentimental loving-kindness of a teacher can be the greatest moral force in the lives of any children outside the home. This may seem like counseling those who teach to steer by the stars, but, to date, the stars, moral or physical, are still mankind's most reliable points of reference.[7]

Proefriedt asks prospective teachers, "Can you devise a way of loving students which will encourage rather than limit the student's growth into a mature human being?" He describes such a love as non-possessive, borrowing C. S. Lewis's phrase "gift love." "We teach them," Lewis says, "in order that they may soon not need our teaching. Then a heavy task is laid

---

6. The phrase "crap detector" is from Postman and Weingartner, *Teaching as a Subversive Activity.*

7. Blakney, "Prime Mover of Youth," 14.

upon this gift love. It must work toward its own abdication. We must aim at making ourselves superfluous."[8]

For Nancy Lou Orth, a retired first grade teacher, the "mother" metaphor is apt.

> The greatest compliment ever paid me, and the most sincere reward I can receive is when a child calls me "Mommy." This indicates to me that when a child can feel that close a relationship with his teacher he must be very happy in his school environment . . . . A really interested teacher cannot be impersonal when dealing with children. That is why my greatest reward in teaching is the privilege of working with children. Their growth and accomplishments are my satisfactions.[9]

I don't need to become Martin's homework-monitoring mom, and my college student never slip up and call me Mom, but I do want to be a woman (old enough to be Martin's mother) who cares whether or not he succeeds this semester. Every few weeks I ask him whether or not he's doing the reading, or if he's studying for the exam earlier than the night before. The answer is sometimes yes, sometimes no, ambivalence that registers on his midterm grade. He starts lingering to tell me about his lacrosse season. "Lacrosse?" I reply. "There's a ball, right? What do you do with it?"

He explains, with the smile that the young reserve for their slow-witted elders, and invites me to a game later in the season. It's still winter weather now, he says, and he doesn't want me to be too cold. I go to a game and am blown away by Martin's skill, intelligence, and endurance. The outcome in my class is as uncertain as in a lacrosse game, but still, I determine to help him parlay those abilities into his academic life.

> Love is something that is so divine
> Love is a feeling that's a friend of mine
> It can't be measured by no sign
> In your heart or even in your mind
>
> —Al Green, *L-O-V-E*

8. Lewis, *Four Loves*, 76.
9. Orth, "I Like Teaching," 170.

In a gender studies seminar we began discussion of love and romance by watching Al Green perform "L-O-V-E" on a 1975 episode of *Soul Train*. Bounding across the stage in a plaid suit jacket and wide white tie, Green exudes so much happiness that students couldn't help but smile and move a little. I wrote metaphors for love on the board as he sang them: love is a walk down Main Street, an apple that is so sweet, a flower in my soul, and a story that can't be told. It's what the world is made of. After the song, I asked:

- *What rings true about these descriptions of love, and where do they fall short?*

- *How do you know what love is?*

Students easily identify the American romantic ideal of love. Love is supposedly an irresistible feeling that is so ephemeral it can't even be described. A person just can't help himself when love overtakes him. Tantalizing as it may be to be swept away by love, many students said they want more from their love relationships than flowers in their souls. They want, eventually, commitment, a life shared together, conflict resolution, maybe even marriage and/or children. They wondered about love's broader realms: what about love of family, nation, humanity, or the planet?

As my students knew, the very long walk down Main Street also includes despair, rage, listlessness, and longing, passions often incited by the very person or entity you're seeking to love. Similarly, developmental psychologist Arthur Jersild explored the "strivings, satisfactions, hopes, and heartaches that pervade the teacher's life and work."[10]

> To say that hostility enters so freely into the life of the scholar and the teacher is not to find fault . . . . The blinder our hostility is, the harsher we are likely to be with others and with ourselves. The more courage and humility we can bring to bear in facing our hostility, the less destructive it is likely to be.[11]

Passion is a word often used to describe the motivation of highly educated people who choose meaningful work that isn't very lucrative. "Well, at least you're passionate about what you do," sighs a wealthy family member discouraged by my outdated home décor. "Passion" means endurance, misery, and hurt. Its sexual implication is a modern addition.[12] Whether erotic or

10. Ibid., 1.

11. Jersild, *When Teachers Face Themselves*, 117.

12. Online Etymology Dictionary, "Passion."

vocational, extreme desire and agitation isn't just simple sensory intensity; it's a complex mix of pleasure and pain, at some level a misery. *Compassion* adds the word "with" (*com*): to suffer with. In describing the inner life of teachers, Jersild continues:

> The compassionate person is not just one who goes out in a good-hearted manner to someone who is having a tough time. He loves, but also hates. He partakes in courage, but also in fear. He partakes in joy, but also in grief. The compassionate person is not just one who goes about with sweet emotions, for he also enters into life's harshness and bitterness. The range of compassion is the range of human emotion.[13]

Love without compassion is mere sweetness. Compassion goes the distance, suffering with, and at times because of, the commitments we've made. Teachers suffer with students in the most costly and practical way when they die because of, or place of, their students. A public school teacher told me about a lockdown at her school. The threat came at lunchtime and as procedure dictated, kids filed into designated classrooms. For two hours she looked after 150 kids packed into a classroom built for thirty. When the gunman, a middle school student, broke a window and smashed his way into a different classroom filled with students, the teacher took a step forward and said gently, "How can I help you?"

The gunman left the room and walked down the hallway, where he found the principal walking toward him, also gently, offering to help. The student fired at the principal and missed. The incident ended without bloodshed.

We can't know what we would do in a life-threatening situation, but most encounters with offensive, unpleasant students are not life-threatening. They threaten to consume our time, grate on our nerves, or push our buttons, and we are faced with the choice of whether or not we are willing to suffer with, and because of, our most repellant students. A loving teacher—which the best of us are only some of the time—greets her offensive students with a sincere and gentle offer, "How can I help you?"

A loving teacher is anything but domesticated; rather, he is radicalized, positioned for action that is patient, kind, gentle, and understanding. A loving teacher becomes the change.

---

13. Jersild, *When Teachers Face Themselves*, 126.

Falling in love is often taken to be serendipitous, exclusive, and special: the love of *eros*. Philosopher Martin Buber distinguishes between erotic love and love suited for education. "Eros is choice, choice made from an inclination. This is precisely what education is not. The man who is living in eros chooses the beloved, the modern educator finds his pupil there before him."[14]

Being a loving teacher is not about choice, inclination, exclusivity, or serendipity; rather, it is loving each student we find before us. We can take this up as a practice. It begins by asking, "How can I see to it that the form my caring takes contributes to the intellectual and moral autonomy of my students?"[15] We can make a habit of falling in love, letting ourselves go toward something so divine, toward love that suffers with, endures, and holds out hope that our highest educational ideals—truth, justice, beauty, goodness—are real and practical. Toward loving compassion that can hold the full range of human passion, even rage, betrayal, and disappointment, neither minimizing them nor giving them center stage. Toward gift love that is self-abdicating.

Letting ourselves love at school means to love and be loved by students, to love our work, and even to have loving compassion toward the systems we work within; that is, to suffer *with* them, not just *within* them. First Corinthians 13 continues,

> Love is patient, love is kind. It does not envy, it does not boast, it is not proud.
> It does not dishonor others, it is not self-seeking, it is not easily angered, it keeps no record of wrongs.
> Love does not delight in evil but rejoices with the truth.
> It always protects, always trusts, always hopes, always perseveres.
> Love never fails (I Cor 13:4–8a, NIV).

14. Buber, *Between Man and Man*, 94.
15. Proefriedt, *Teacher You Choose to Be*, 60.

Epilogue
Commencing

Beginnings are often laden with fear, perhaps because they touch on the sacred. In the Bible, the phrase "Fear not!" appears dozens of times, when the sacred moves through the world in a new way. For example, when angels announce Jesus' birth to some shepherds, they lead with, "Fear not!"

Whether we are beginning our first year of teaching or our forty-first, there may be a tinge of fear, or even something stronger such as dread or panic. Some of my fears show their faces in late August back-to-school dreams. My kindergarten dream self hid under her desk in shame, realizing too late she'd forgotten to put on a shirt. Ten-year-old me was late for class and without her books, frantically opening and shutting lockers down an endless hallway in a fruitless attempt to locate her backpack. In high school I was the debate team champion, struck speechless in a final round as an audience of thousands stared. This year, nearly two decades into a teaching career, my dream self is a professor of anthropology wandering the halls of my college in a panic. I can't find my classroom. I've lost my books. I can't remember the subject of the class. These dreams all end the same way, with a quick awakening and a grateful realization, "It was only a dream!" And then I head off for school.

If only our fears were mere dreams; our anxieties over funding, technology, testing, and guns are very much grounded in reality. Even in the best of times, however, education and fear are closely linked. In Plato's "Allegory of the Cave," a group of people live chained inside a cave, facing a wall. They see shadows projected onto the wall by a fire behind them, and mistake the shadows for reality. The philosopher—for our purposes, any educated person—escapes the cave and comes to see the shadows as shadows, and reality as reality.

His escape is dangerous because most people prefer their chains to the struggle for freedom, and they don't believe there is anything more real than the shadows. His life may well be at stake:

> Wouldn't he remember his first home, what passed for wisdom there, and his fellow prisoners, and consider himself happy and them pitiable? And wouldn't he disdain whatever honors, praises, and prizes were awarded there to the ones who guessed best which shadows followed which? Moreover, were he to return there, wouldn't he be rather bad at their game, no longer being accustomed to the darkness? Wouldn't it be said of him that he went up and came back with his eyes corrupted, and that it's not even worth trying to go up? And if they were somehow able to get their hands on the man who attempts to release and lead them up, wouldn't they kill him?[1]

For the teacher, education is about convincing students to free themselves, to prefer reality over shadow, and to work hard to ascend to a clearer view of the world and of themselves. For students, it's about choosing to begin the ascent.

When I started kindergarten, I cried so often I had to take a note home each day to my mom, telling her whether or not I had cried.

When my mom asked, "Why do you cry?" I'd whimper.

When my teacher, Miss Brilia, asked, "What's wrong?" I'd fall silent.

I feared many things, and I remember them still:

- Our name tags were color coded, and I got a color that didn't match my personality.

- The bathroom stalls didn't have doors, so you'd have to take a friend with you to "guard"; that is, stand with her back to you while you went. We were all afraid of having to go number two during school hours.

- Miss Brilia asked me how high I could count. Instead of answering, I just started counting: one–two–three–four–five. She made me stop at one hundred, but I could count higher, and she would never know.

---

1. This translation is from Leshem-Gradus, "Fine Arts." For full text, see Plato, *The Republic*, 257.

My friend cried, too. She said it was because Miss Brilia's head was too oval.

Starting school—commencing—takes a child away from her home into the broader world of name tags, new bathrooms, and women whose heads look different than Mom's. Those fears are perhaps an inkling that education is moving us away from what we've known and who we have been.

The prisoner in the cave risks his life to see reality as it truly is. He has to overcome both his self-delusion and fear and the hatred of his companions. Paulo Freire describes Brazilian peasants and other oppressed people as having internalized the values and views of their oppressors. "The oppressed . . . are fearful of freedom. Freedom would require them to eject this image and replace it with autonomy and responsibility. Freedom is acquired by conquest, not by gift. It must be pursued constantly and responsibly."[2]

In Freire's view, everyone needs liberation, oppressed and oppressor alike. The oppressor class is too invested in material and ideological privilege, so the oppressed must lead. They can overcome their fear of freedom, their love of staring at shadows on the wall, through literacy and basic education that is grounded in their lived experience. This is a struggle that their teachers forge *with* them, not *for* them. It is a struggle that is worth the effort because it will liberate not only the individual, but communities and societies.

True, too, for a suburban American girl. Miss Brilia couldn't stop me from crying, accommodate my favorite colors, or redesign the school bathrooms. She didn't do any of this *for* me, but she was a creative, bright, instructive teacher who was *with* me as I struggled toward freedom. That's not putting it too strongly: as a five year old in the late 1970s, I didn't face murder by peers, as Plato warned, nor the political repression, poverty, or illiteracy faced by Third World peasants. I was, however, already deeply programmed for a life of consumerism, racial superiority, nationalism, and self-centeredness. All students are "at risk"; the risks differ with context, but are always present.

I couldn't put any of this into words, but my fears were a true flag of warning: learning would change my life. I begged my older sister to teach me whatever was happening in the grade above me, so I'd know it before I got there. I annoyed my teachers by working too quickly and asking for

2. Freire, *Pedagogy of the Oppressed*, 29.

more. I weaseled my way into the librarian's heart so she'd let me skip recess and help her shelve books.

Every year until third or fourth grade, I cried on the first day of school. Every year my mom would ask, "Why?" and I'd have no answer. But by late September, every single year, love would prove stronger than fear. The new library books, the lure of starting in on integers, or the challenge of memorizing state capitals, would win me over. I loved school so much I never left; since kindergarten, I've had no more than a summer's break between school years.

For most students, though, school eventually ends. Graduates end by beginning; that is, commencing. My college seniors are stressed, rushing through final exams, begging for extra credit, searching for summer housing, hoping for jobs or graduate school acceptances, and enjoying last parties, last games of Frisbee golf, and last tube floats down the campus creek.

Every spring I say good-bye to students I've come to treasure. I think about how some will spend their summers, their romances, or the rest of their lives. I remember some great class sessions from that year, and also regret some books I assigned, and some murkily designed assignments. I revisit the decisions I made in the spring of my own senior year: not to marry *him*, to go to graduate school now instead of later, to become an anthropologist and not an economist or a journalist. I wonder who I might have become, and who I am becoming; that is, what is commencing for me.

And there are balloons. In high school they were orange and black (go Orioles!). College, blue and yellow (go Royals!). Graduate school, red white and blue (go Eagles!). Now, blue and white (go Falcons!).

If you're going to spend forty years of your life as a teacher, it makes sense to do some serious thinking about the kind of teacher you wish to become. The problem is not only to decide at what grade level you wish to teach or in which subject area to specialize; more fundamentally, you must choose the role which you will take in this society, at this point in history. Too many teachers before you have floated through their careers without ever questioning the nature of the life they have chosen.

—William Proefriedt[3]

---

3. Proefriedt, *Teacher You Choose To Be*, 1.

When I started teaching, my balloons of idealism were my own, un-tethered and pure: I wanted to do meaningful work, love and be loved by students, and receive a measure of respect from society. That was a long time ago. These days, balloons like that don't float down from the sky into my open hands.

Each spring as I sit on the soccer-field-turned-graduation-venue, decked out in regalia, following along in my program as the names of hundreds of graduates are read in turn, I look off toward the parking lot where cookies are served and families greet educators, and see balloons waving. These balloons are purchased on a college budget line, tied and taken outside by event planners, and taken down after the event on a carefully planned schedule. They are tethered to this place, and so am I. *This* school, with its strengths and its flaws. *This* sector of the economy, lumbering into the future irrationally committed to its business model. *This* time, full of terrorism and violence and economic insecurity and a hundred other good reasons to be afraid. *This* body, *this* brain, *this* PhD, with all I can offer and all that I can't.

If I'm going to be happy and whole, it needs to be here. Taking the classroom as a sacred space, and teaching as a holy pursuit, casts the quotidian tasks of teaching in a new light. Spirited teaching releases the *animus* of each student, each book and notebook, and each class session. Taking up the ordinary elements of teaching as spiritual practices makes us more open to change and growth. Even as we grow to become master teachers, we remain apprentices in the tradition of pursuing wisdom, love, and beauty in the world as it is.

Was that commencement speaker right about fear and love? He proclaimed, "Perfect love casts out fear." Many teachers were perfectionist students—I certainly was—and might take this to mean that we ought never be afraid, and if we are, we've failed to love perfectly. Now we're afraid of failing to love correctly, which only adds to the list of fears that love was supposed to cast out.

When I tracked my highs and lows, when I tried to pay attention in class to all that was happening there, including in my own heart and spirit, I found more imperfection than perfection, and I more often found my fears reduced, not cast out. If perfect love casts out fear, perhaps ordinary love diminishes fear.

I see that balloon, its string dangling down within reach.

I've stayed in touch with Dr. Stone, my favorite philosophy professor. Years afterward, I showed him the photo of myself behind his desk, the one I had my friend snap when the professor was out of his office. I was his student in the middle years of his career: he had been teaching twenty years before I came along, and for twenty-five more years after.

At a college homecoming event, a small group of my college friends joined Dr. Stone for dinner and dessert, drawing out his life story and asking lingering questions we had about Kierkegaard and Nietzsche. He complimented us effusively, not for our beauty or our personalities, but for our questions. "So smart, this one! Did you hear her question?" "Beautiful question!" "Just lovely, how you thought about that!"

I knew he had emeritus status and no longer worked from the office he'd used for forty-five years. I asked, "When was it that you retired from teaching?"

He laughed, "Well, the college says I retired ten years ago. But I'm still reading, still learning. And am I not teaching you right now?"

Bibliography

"African Wedding." http://www.huffingtonpost.com/2013/12/10/african-wedding_n _4421604.html.

American Anthropological Association. "American Anthropological Association Statement of Ethics." http://aaanet.org/stmts/ethstmnt.htm.

Blakney, Raymond. "The Prime Mover of Youth." In *Why Teach?*, edited by D. Louise Sharp, 13–14. New York: Henry Holt, 1957.

Brookfield, Stephen. *The Skillful Teacher: On Technique, Trust, and Responsiveness in the Classroom.* San Francisco: Jossey-Bass, 1990.

Browning, Dan. "Archdiocese Insider Battles Catholic Church over Sex Abuse." *StarTribune,* October 15, 2013. http://www.startribune.com/oct-13-insider-battles-archdiocese-over-sex-abuse/227537151/.

Buber, Martin. *Between Man and Man.* Boston: Beacon, 1955.

Chagnon, Napoleon A. *Yąnomamö: The Fierce People.* New York: Holt, Rinehart and Winston, 1983.

Davis, Stephen, Patrick Drinan, and Tricia Bertram Gallant. *Cheating in School: What We Know and What We Can Do.* Malden, MA: Wiley-Blackwell, 2009.

Dykstra, Craig, and Dorothy C. Bass. *Practicing our Faith: A Way of Life for a Searching People.* San Francisco: Jossey-Bass, 2010.

Emerson, Ralph Waldo. "Spiritual Laws." In *Essays, First Series.* 1841. Reprint, The Literature Page, http://www.literaturepage.com/read/emersonessays1-73.html.

Freire, Paulo. *Pedagogy of the Oppressed.* New York: Herder and Herder, 1970.

———. *Teachers as Cultural Workers: Letters to Those Who Dare Teach.* Boulder, CO: Westview, 1998.

Fried, Robert L. *The Passionate Teacher: A Practical Guide.* Boston: Beacon, 1995.

Fuller, Frances F., "Intensive Individualization of Teacher Preparation." In *The Teacher as a Person*, edited by Luiz F. S. Natalicio and Carl F. Hereford, 1–26. Dubuque, IA: W. C. Brown, 1971.

Hanh, Thich Nhat, and Robert Ellsberg. *Thich Nhat Hanh: Essential Writings.* Maryknoll, NY: Orbis, 2001.

Hanh, Thich Nhat, and Rachel Neumann. *Calming the Fearful Mind: A Zen Response to Terrorism.* Berkeley: Parallax, 2005.

Heclo, Hugh. *On Thinking Institutionally.* Boulder, CO: Paradigm, 2008.

hooks, bell. *Teaching to Transgress: Education as the Practice of Freedom*. New York: Routledge, 1994.

Intrator, Sam M. *Stories of the Courage to Teach: Honoring the Teacher's Heart*. San Francisco: Jossey-Bass, 2002.

Jersild, Arthur T. *When Teachers Face Themselves*. New York: Teachers College, 1955.

June, Audrey Williams. "Budget Cuts and 'Workload Creep.'" *The Chronicle of Higher Education*, September 7, 2009. http://chronicle.com/article/More-Work-Can-Mean-Less-Joy-in/48309.

Katz, Richard, Megan Biesele, and Verna St. Denis. *Healing Makes Our Hearts Happy: Spirituality and Cultural Transformation among the Kalahari Ju/'hoansi*. Rochester, VT: Inner Traditions, 1997.

Lang, James M. *Cheating Lessons: Learning from Academic Dishonesty*. Cambridge, MA: Harvard University Press, 2013.

Lears, Jackson. "Reform of the Reform: How Not to Fix our Schools." *Commonweal*, November 15 (2013) 23–28.

Lee, Richard. *Dobe Ju/'hoansi*. Belmont, CA: Wadsworth Cengage Learning, 2013.

Leshem-Gradus, Noa. "Fine Arts." http://noaleshemgradus.com/platos-cave.

Levy, David M. "No Time to Think: Reflections on Information Technology and Contemplative Scholarship." *Ethics and Information Technology* 9 (2007) 237–249.

Lewis, C. S. *The Four Loves*. New York: Hartcourt Brace Jovanovich, 1960.

Lichtmann, Maria R. *The Teacher's Way: Teaching and the Contemplative Life*. New York: Paulist, 2005.

Mauss, Marcel. *The Gift: Forms and Functions of Exchange in Archaic Societies*. New York: W. W. Norton, 1967.

Menzies, Heather. *No Time: Stress and the Crisis of Modern Life*. Vancouver, BC: Douglas & McIntyre, 2005.

Miller, Karen Maezen. *Momma Zen: Walking the Crooked Path of Motherhood*. Boston: Shambhala, 2006.

Molloff, Jeanine. "*Waiting for Superman* is an Insult to True Educators." *Huffington Post*, September 21, 2010. http://www.huffingtonpost.com/jeanine-molloff/waiting-for-superman-film_b_733094.html.

Movie Fanatic. http://www.moviefanatic.com/quotes/we-are-the-borg-lower-your-shields-and-surrender-your-ships-we-w/.

Natalicio, Luiz F. S., and Carl F. Hereford. *The Teacher as a Person*. Dubuque, IA: W. C. Brown, 1971.

"A Nation at Risk." http://www2.ed.gov/pubs/NatAtRisk/risk.html.

"National Poll on Children's Health." http://mottnpch.org/.

Newman, Barbara. "The Contemplative Classroom, or Learning by Heart in the Age of Google." *Buddhist-Christian Studies* 33 (2013) 3–11.

O'Reilley, Mary Rose. *The Garden at Night: Burnout and Breakdown in the Teaching Life*. Portsmouth, NH: Heinemann, 2005.

———. *Radical Presence: Teaching as Contemplative Practice*. Portsmouth, NH: Boynton/Cook, 1998.

Online Etymology Dictionary. "Attend." http://www.etymonline.com/index.php?term=attend.

———. "Apprentice." http://etymonline.com/?term=apprentice.

———. "Integrity." http://www.etymonline.com/index.php?term=integrity.

———. "Passion." http://www.etymonline.com/index.php?term=passion.

Orth, Nancy Lou. "I Like Teaching." In *Why Teach?*, edited by D. Louise Sharp, 169–70. New York: Henry Holt, 1957.

Palmer, Parker J. "Good Teaching: A Matter of Living the Mystery." *Change* 22:1(1990) 10–16.

———. "Teaching with Heart and Soul: Reflections on Spirituality in Teacher Education." *Journal of Teacher Education* 54:5 (2003) 376–85.

———. *To Know As We Are Known: A Spirituality of Education.* San Francisco: Harper & Row, 1983.

Parrillo, Vincent. *Understanding Race and Ethnic Relations.* 2nd ed. Boston, MA: Pearson, 2005.

Peck, M. Scott. *The Different Drum: Community-Making and Peace.* New York: Simon and Schuster, 1987.

Plato. *The Republic.* Translated by Benjamin Jowett. New York: The Modern Library, 1941.

Postman, Neil. *The End of Education: Redefining the Value of School.* New York: Knopf, 1995.

Postman, Neil, and Charles Weingartner. *Teaching as a Subversive Activity.* New York: Delacorte, 1969.

Proefriedt, William. *The Teacher You Choose to Be.* New York: Holt, Rinehart and Winston, 1974.

Psychology Foundation of Canada. "Booklet for Parents." http://psychologyfoundation. org/.

"Race to the Top Executive Summary." http://www2.ed.gov/programs/racetothetop/ executive-summary.pdf.

Roewe, Brian. "Former Minnesota Archdiocean Official Shines a Light on Failures." *National Catholic Reporter,* October 21, 2013. http://ncronline.org/news/ accountability/shining-light-failures.

Rogers, Carl. "The Characteristics of a Helping Relationship." *The Personnel and Guidance Journal* 37(1958) 6–16.

———. "Significant Learning: In Therapy and Education." In *The Teacher as a Person*, edited by Luiz F. S. Natalicio and Carl F. Hereford, 106–7. Dubuque, IA: W. C. Brown, 1971.

Rotne, Nikolaj Flor, and Didde Flor Rotne, *Everybody Present: Mindfulness in Education.* Berkeley, CA: Parallax, 2013.

Sahlins, Marshall. *Stone Age Economics.* Chicago: Aldine-Atherton, 1972.

Shostak, Marjorie. *Nisa: The Life and Words of a !Kung Woman.* Cambridge, MA: Harvard University Press, 1981.

Shteir, Rachel. "MOOCs and the Arts: A Plea for Slow Education." *The Chronicle Review,* July 8, 2013. http://chronicle.com/article/MOOCsthe-Arts-A-Plea-for/140119/.

Taylor, June. "What is artisinal food?" http://blog.sfgate.com/stockdale/2009/10/30/what-is-artisanal-food/.

Thwaites, Thomas. *The Toaster Project: Or a Heroic Attempt to Build a Simple Electric Appliance from Scratch.* New York: Princeton Architectural, 2011.

Tolle, Eckhart. *Practicing the Power of Now: Essential Teachings, Meditations, and Exercises from the Power of Now.* Novato, CA: New World Library, 1999.

———. *Stillness Speaks: Whispers of Now.* Novato, CA: New World Library and Namaste, 2003.

Ulich, Robert, ed. *Three Thousand Years of Educational Wisdom: Selections from Great Documents.* Cambridge, MA: Harvard University Press, 1947.

Van Der Werf, Martin, and Grant Sabatier. *The College of 2020: Students*. Washington, DC: Chronicle Research Services, 2009.

Van Dyke, Henry. "The Unknown Teacher." In *Why Teach?*, edited by D. Louise Sharp, iv. New York: Henry Holt, 1957.

Weil, Simone. *Waiting for God*. New York: Harper & Row, 1973.

Wikipedia, "Lemming." http://en.wikipedia.org/wiki/Lemming.

Made in the USA
Middletown, DE
17 October 2018